DEDICATION

For you
born in the in-between
born to bridge worlds

Let us create new worlds
together

TABLE OF CONTENTS

FOREWORD
By Julia Stege

A most magical turn of events brought Sophia Remolde and me together and led to me writing the foreword to this book.

As the founder of Magical Marketing Company, I have spent years helping spiritual business women and conscious entrepreneurs to clarify and express their purpose through branding and websites that attract their perfect customers online...magically!

A few years ago, Sophia got a copy of my book, *Branding from the Heart: How to Share Your Purpose through Marketing that Attracts Your Tribe and Inspires a Revolution* and read it cover to cover. She felt a special resonance with me and stayed connected through my email list. When I promoted one of my online communities, she decided to join, and came to the live event. I was there, but we hadn't met yet when Sophia stood in front of the room and told the story of Lobsterbird and shared about serving change-makers.

Out of over 300 people, I recognized her right away as someone I wanted to meet so I made sure she was invited to dinner with some friends and me. While we were sharing stories and connecting, Sophia let me know I had inspired her to be there! It felt like a deep confirmation of my work, and Sophia said, "Our meeting basically proves your book right—that getting aligned with your purpose and clarifying your soul tribe attracts them to you."

We have become fast cohorts and friends, and I am proud of the work Sophia is doing to share the magic and start a revolution of creative enlightenment for those who are suffering in cubicle-land, stuck in jobs they hate.

With this book, you are about to embark on a fantastic and revelatory journey within. Have you ever wondered:

- Is there is more to life than this?
- What is my purpose?

or

- Should I be doing something else?

You are not alone. A recent Gallup poll reveals that 85% of people worldwide admit to hating their jobs. That means that overall, only fifteen percent of workers feel engaged by their work. According to Forbes, "engaged" means that they feel a sense of passion for and deep connection to their work, spending their days driving innovation and moving their company forward.

Are you in the wrong camp? If you have picked up this book, odds are that you suspect your life could have a lot more meaning than it currently does, if only you could find your calling.

Then rejoice that you have found this book, because now you no longer need to suffer along with the masses of uninspired, disengaged workers. You now have the transformative guidebook that can change your life.

Sophia Remolde uses Joseph Campbell's famous "Hero's Journey" as the structure to guide you out of your Ordinary World and into a daring adventure, one where you can find your true purpose and passion and seize your just reward: engaging in work that satisfies you at the core and changes the world.

Sophia is an expert in this arena as she also experienced the vast emptiness that stalked her as she sought to discover her place in the world. In order to help people overcome disempowering circumstances and experience meaningful lives, Sophia pursued multiple conventional and nonconventional career trajectories.

After working many jobs that were out of alignment and suffering severe burnout, a liberation occurred. These seemingly disparate paths merged together and guided Sophia all over the world, creating art, engaging in Compassionate Social Action projects, and ultimately creating her program, *The Hero's Way*. She now trains others to align their own experiences and abilities into work that has a positive impact on this planet.

Phase Out follows Sophia's real-world pilgrimage from the Void into the Light, outlining the steps along her Hero's Journey and offering tools for the reader to join her in their own virtual pilgrimage, where you too can answer the call to adventure, conquer the enemies of shadow, bust through the myths of Ordinary World, and unearth your rightful treasure.

Sophia is a natural storyteller, relating her perspective from the nitty-gritty earth realm, to the magical and fantastical, to the science of quantum mechanics. Her energy, experience, and wisdom shine, and yet this roadmap is fun and easy to read. This is your invitation to change your story, re-write your happy ending, oh, and save the planet too!

The life you crave is closer than you might think. This book will help you to simplify the logistics of what is keeping you stuck. It is a practical guide to finding the work you were born to do, starting with all the tools you have at your disposal. If you don't know what those are, then *Phase Out* is a must-read. I am sure that Sophia's book will inspire spiritual and socially conscious creatives around the world to action, uniting our tribes and inciting a revolution that will create the world we desire.

Now is your time more than ever. With all of the changes going on in technology, the environment, and politics, we have never had a greater responsibility and opportunity to make a difference. I recommend that you turn these pages, and allow this book to transform your life, and the world.

Julia Stege
The Magical Marketer
www.Magical-Marketing.com
Author of *Branding from the Heart: How to Share Your Purpose through Marketing that Attracts Your Tribe and Inspires a Revolution*

INTRODUCTION

"Life is either a daring adventure or nothing. To keep our faces toward change and behave like free spirits in the presence of fate is strength undefeatable."

—**Helen Keller**

Ordinary World: Your Job is Your Life

The majority of people on this planet are not doing work they love. If you fall into this category, you are definitely not alone.

As one example, Gallup has been measuring international employee satisfaction since the 1990s. They report that only 13% of workers worldwide feel engaged by their jobs. 87% of people in the world do not feel connected to their work.

I imagine this on a spectrum. Like the make-up of our universe itself, there are polarities. At -10, we have "I hate my job and either want to quit or die." At +10, we have "I love my job and would never choose to do anything other than what I am doing in this moment." In between the two, we have a neutral 0, something akin to "I don't love my job or hate it. Sometimes it's boring and stresses me out, but I have health insurance and two weeks of paid vacation each year. I'm not super inspired, but at least I have a job."

From my personal experience and observations of meeting people around the globe and delving deeply into the topic of "love for life," I would say 99.9% of people are working somewhere along 5 to -10 on the Job Love Meter.

Where are you along this scale?

Most of the people I know are hovering somewhere in the middle. I've had countless dear friends and family members come to me complaining about their jobs, as if they were stuck in some kind of life-sucking vortex that seemed impossible to escape from. After graduating college, I noted, "The mantra of our generation is: 'I hate my job. I hate my job.'" No one seemed happy, myself included. Even when I felt happy and was doing what I loved, I was living under the constant threat of financial instability. I was working too hard and burning out on a regular basis. Most ominously, I wasn't entirely sure I was contributing to the good of humanity on a larger scale. Definitely not a +10 on the Job Love Meter.

This pervasive dread is the insistent undercurrent to our lives. It's like the crime networks below the city streets, causing harm whose source no one can detect.

We went into university with bright eyes and big dreams, not even necessarily knowing what we would be when we came out. But one thing felt certain—college was an opportunity that many generations of our ancestors never had before. It promised a well-oiled system that we could plug ourselves into and find lucrative work on the other side.

And many of us did. Some became copywriters, worked in finance, managed university offices within our alma mater. They were doing fine. But the world changed a lot in a few short years. More and more people were emerging with degrees. It took even more school and more advanced degrees to get the really good positions–to become professors, CEOs, or start one's own practice. This group with "good jobs" had health insurance and the potential to work their way up the proverbial ladder. But inside their hearts, they were yearning for something more.

Others opted for a different route, deciding to become actors, writers, or artists. It seemed like the rebel thing to do, but lo and behold, they were still bound by a system that depended on working their way up to some impossible position. (Your entire career hinged on who you knew to get you published, on stage, or in a gallery–notably the people that had the most money and connections.) Busting their buns for years on end to achieve the dream of making it big and "being discovered" meant working jobs that often had nothing to do with their passion and certainly didn't provide the means to live in prosperity.

I was in this latter camp. From the outside, life may have looked different, pseudo-glamorous even. However, the same problem remained: We lived in a world that did not support us in doing what we loved and we wanted something more. But how could we phase out of jobs we had committed to and take leaps of faith into lives we loved that didn't yet exist? Was it even possible in this world to live a creative life where we felt connected to a sense of meaning and direction?

When I was sixteen, I read the book *A Child Named It*. I was struck by this tale of horror, abuse, perseverance, and transcendence. I decided as I turned the last page, that I wanted to help people overcome their disempowered circumstances to experience meaningful lives. So I went to Rutgers University to study child psychology. I had it all mapped out: I would go to college and become a child psychologist. Start helping people when they're young so they can grow up to save us all. The world would become a better place.

Yet Rutgers was huge and overwhelming. There were 450 kids in my general psych class, the equivalent of my entire high school graduating class. While the numbers dwindled as the courses became more specialized, the treatment for the problems never proved transformative. For the more severe illnesses in Abnormal Psych, the answer was always prescribing medication to dull the symptoms. It didn't seem to get to the source of the pain. For general life problems, getting to the root of the issue meant blaming someone or something— the parents, or past experience, or a flaw within a person's psyche. Where was the middle road?

After getting my degree early, I quit psychology (to the heartbreak of my parents). I went to study art in Florence, Italy, and decided to move to New York City to become an actor. In New York, I discovered post-modern theater and started making my own art. Eventually I got an MFA in performance and technology, and got trapped in yet again another system: the art world.

But at least I was living a creative life, right? I was free compared to my companions that were stuck in an office all day.

Wrong! I was bartending to pay my exorbitant NYC rent and burning myself out by working on performance projects while staying up late nights to sling drinks. I loved my many jobs, actually. I worked in the most fun music clubs and karaoke bars in the city, and couldn't have asked for a better situation. Except to not be working in bars at all. At the time, I couldn't imagine what it would be like to *only* do what I loved and have that support me fully.

In the meantime, I never really gave up on psychology. Three of my closest friends were in situation #1 with "normal jobs." And they were pretty miserable. So I was working on creating a program that would use their inherent creativity to free them from the confines of their cubicles.

They were all intelligent, creative, caring souls who deserved to be doing whatever the heck they wanted. Only they didn't know what that was. I vowed to help them find it, and spent years researching creativity and psychology, and developing my "Human Potential Project."

But here's the thing about the world we were raised in–it did not empower us to understand that our creativity was our sole currency. It did not preach about powers that would conspire to help us find and fulfill our life's purpose. So we took jobs we didn't want while we hoped for a way out.

Does this resonate? And what will it take for us to wake up and change those numbers? How can we move from the -10 of Job Misery to loving our work at a +10?

Can you imagine if 99.9% of the world was doing work they truly loved? Wouldn't a natural side-effect be less stress and more happiness? Wouldn't you feel like you were doing good work if you were contributing your natural gifts to generating abundance for yourself and world peace for all?

That may seem like a far stretch if you are mired in the bog of "I hate my job." But the world has changed a lot since we entered the workforce. Modern technology has increased our ability to connect and create on levels our ancestors could have never imagined. We can go anywhere and do anything, and the internet is at work to truly democratize our ability to earn. You can set up shop online in minutes, reaching people all over the world who want what you have to give. I understand that it's not so easy to quit the life we built for ourselves. Mastering technology might be easy for the digital natives who were born with an iPad in their hands. But those of us born before the advent of the internet occupy an important role in bridging the material realm with that of unlimited possibility. It is up to us to generate a level playing field by evolving the current systems, while embracing the incoming energy that will create a whole new world.

My studies in spirituality and science tell me that everything is ready to create this world. The notion of universal co-creation was once relegated to spiritual philosophy and mysticism. However, modern science is coming out with radical new discoveries every day that prove these ancient spiritual ideas are actually true.

We simply have to change our way of thinking. It's both the easiest and hardest thing we could do. It may seem difficult because we've been conditioned by cultures that prize competition over creativity. That darkness would have us believe that there are only a certain number of jobs or only certain ways to "get to the top." It was easy to see how you go to college, get an internship at a company, get an entry-level job, work your way up to a management position, and possibly become a CEO of a company (and more likely so if you fit a certain demographic). You would find the perfect partner and have 2.5 kids, and because of your good job with health insurance and benefits, everything would work out and you would be happy and healthy, and then die. It's not easy to find the guiding light amidst this darkness because it's hidden inside us and all around us. However, the light is right there, waiting for the moment when it can explode into a beacon of clarity for all who wish to see it.

There is a danger to keeping your eyes shut when this light calls you to see it. This book is one of those calls. It's like the Bat-Signal–are you willing to let Gotham fall to the throes of anarchy, abuse, and despair because you're not willing to put on your utility belt and get to work ridding the city of evil?

If you don't absolutely love going to work, then isn't your intuition telling you it's not the work for you? If you had complete certainty that the Bat-Signal was calling you, and only you, to save the city, would you do it? Wouldn't you feel your sense of purpose, knowing it is work that only *you* can do?

If you feel that spark lighting up your heart that signals the hope of another way, if a burning in your gut is telling you to read on, if there's a voice whispering *"yes"* and you can just barely make it out, then turn the page and meet your destiny. This book will guide you out of the job that is slowly sucking your soul. It will provide you with a clear path to discover the work you are meant to do. Everything you have done up until this point has prepared you for this moment. You will synthesize every experience and transmute it all into a new way of working. A new way of being. And you will learn to use your creativity to create a better world for all.

Get ready for a Hero's Journey without even needing to leave home!

Chapter 1

DO YOU HEAR THE CALL?

"Nothingness is your ending; Why, then, are you living?"
—**Kahlil Gibran**

The Call to Adventure

Have you ever seen *The NeverEnding Story?*

In this epic movie, the main character Bastian is a seemingly normal kid. Maybe he's a little shy and bookish, and that's enough to make the school bullies chase him until he has to hide in a dumpster. Finding himself at such a low, disgusting level, however, is exactly what leads him to his destiny. He is guided to a mystical bookshop where the snarky shopkeeper cautions him not to read a tantalizing book–a tale of danger and adventure meant exactly for him to find.

Bastian takes the book and hides out in the school's creepy basement while a storm rages around him. He delves into this new world. In this Special World, there is a dark force called "The Nothing" that is sweeping the land of Fantasia, threatening to annihilate the entire universe. In some strange way that requires going beyond time, space, and the boundaries of the book's pages, Bastian realizes that the story isn't merely a story. It is up to him to save the day.

The Nothing that threatens to destroy all living things is this dark and powerful current that pervades the human psyche. It manifests in our lives in any number of ways–being bullied, facing poverty, or even working a job you don't like. You hear The Nothing is coming, but how can you fight something that is nothing? So you go about your life, riding snails who are blissfully eating grass, while The Nothing sweeps its way across the land. For most people, by the time they realize it's here, it's too late. We must identify this slow monotony of darkness that will take us down the first chance it gets. Then, we must team up to find a way to stop it.

For us on this particular Hero's Journey, The Nothing is the emptiness we feel when we are not fully aligned with work we love. I know it might not seem like much. For many of us, we are grateful to have roofs over our heads, food to eat, and maybe even work that allows us to travel or buy presents for our family on special occasions. I am all about being grateful for what we have in the present moment; these things *are* to be cherished and be thankful for every day. However, that snail practicing ignorance-is-bliss is not going to kick into its high racing gear capacity unless you get in the saddle. Don't mistake gratitude for complacency. The Nothing is a culmination of forces that have oppressed personal empowerment and universal connection for way too long. Now it is out of control. It has caused us to abuse our planet and war against one another. It has created systems and structures that put power in the hands of a limited few. That emptiness you feel when you take time to contemplate your contribution to the world is signaling you to get on that snail. It may seem slow-going at first. But just as The Nothing carries with it its own momentum, so too can the power of people joining together to create work that stirs our souls.

Before we can get to that point, however, we need to look more deeply into ourselves and the roles we have been playing.

My Call to Adventure

I first understood The Nothing was coming when I was in Tokyo, Japan in May 2014. I was there to work with a Japanese Butoh Master on a performance project combining this Japanese perceptual art form with robotics. It was everything I had wanted to do; I had freshly completed my graduate thesis called *Robot Immigrants*, where I combined Butoh and robotics to tell my mother's immigrant story. This was my first time in Japan. My mother was born in Osaka and raised in Korea. It felt like destiny.

But while I was there, my work began to feel strained. I was in a country that was kind of my own, but I could hardly speak to anyone or understand how anything worked. My collaborator was having a really difficult time and was stressful to be around. The work felt forced. It felt like there was a void instead of the ecstatic flow of artmaking. Why wasn't it as magical as it should have been? I had no answers and no language or anyone to speak of it with.

I felt The Nothing coming, but at that point it was a force I couldn't grapple with.

Then, my cousins invited me to visit them in Korea for my birthday. I had never been to Korea either. I was grateful but came up with a million reasons not to go. But my friend Miyu had just found out at age 25 that she was half Korean and immediately flew over there to "check it out."

"You have to go," she said. "You never know when you'll have another chance. And it's right there."

It occurred to me that I would have to fly from Osaka where my mother was born and then go to Seoul where she grew up. I would be following in her footsteps on an ancestral pilgrimage of sorts. I didn't know it, but this would be the first of many pilgrimages to come.

While I was in Seoul, I freed my Soul. For the first time ever, I understood what unconditional love was. I was loved so hard (and fed so much) by this family I had never met before. I couldn't speak to them in Korean, and because The Nothing was coming, I was feeling the misery and despair of having lived most of my life without this kind of unconditional love. As they stuffed me with kimchi and kalbi, the food had nowhere to go except out my eyeballs. I cried the whole time and was a big mess.

Then, The Nothing appeared. I looked at my whole life and every aspect of it from this newfound lens of unconditional love. I realized that 99.9% of my life was not lived with this kind of love. Most notably, I did not love myself. With this realization, it was as if The Nothing started destroying everything dear to me in one fell swoop. Relationships disappeared from my life, my finances were obliterated, my body gave out, and I came back to Tokyo and quit the job I had come for. Anything that did not have that feeling I felt in Seoul had to go. And it did.

I lay on the floor of my Tokyo apartment for weeks as my entire life crumbled. I was paralyzed on the left side of my back and neck, a recurring stress injury from years of pushing my body and working too much. Since I couldn't move, I decided to use this time as an artistic experience. *How far can I let this all go??* My only activity was to breathe, cry, let go, occasionally go to the bathroom or eat, and listen to Alan Watts. The latter came to me days before my decline when my collaborator asked me if I knew who Alan Watts was. I had no idea so I let him come save me in my despair. And he did.

When I could finally move again, I went to see my friend Jyana and found the clue that sent me on a pilgrimage to an alternate reality. When I ended my old life, I gave birth to a new one. On the pilgrimage, I was a disaster. The only direction I had was "get from Temple #1 to Temple #88." And for about 75% of that journey, I wasn't even really there. Most days, I was walking and trapped inside my own head, thinking about what I thought I needed instead of where I actually was. It sounded something like this in there:

I'm hungry. My knee hurts. Where am I going to stay tonight? I wonder if I'll get to the next temple. It's hot. I wish my bag wasn't so heavy. I'm hungry. Should I eat in a restaurant or stop at a convenience store? What if there isn't one for miles? What if I have to sleep outside because I can't find a place to stay? What if there are snakes? My knee hurts. What if it gives out? I'm tired. What am I going to do with my life? Can you believe all that happened? I'm hungry. I have no money. I have no job. What am I doing here???

And so on.

I will never forget the moment when I was crossing through a rice paddy to get to the next temple. I had to walk along the lines of the field, surrounded by pools of water gestating unborn rice and a great deal of mosquitos. It was hot and I was miserable. The rice fields seemed to stretch on as far as the eye could see, a crisscross of the mundane. And I was going through the usual rigmarole inside my head about everything that was wrong or could go wrong. And then it hit me. Like I, this lone pilgrim with my funny hat in the middle of an epic rice field, was a lightning rod.

I stopped walking and looked up. Past the endless rice fields, the earth reached up into the heavens. Everything was illuminated and crystal clear. It was as if I had never seen the sky before. In that moment, nothing else mattered. *My thoughts are the only thing blocking me from divine existence!* Then I started laughing, by myself, in the middle of an endless expanse. I cut through the fabric of a false reality that I had constructed as my life. I also knew that if I could do that pilgrimage, I could do anything. I could create a whole new life.

When I came back from the pilgrimage, I was changed. I could see things more clearly, as if I were writing my life story with every step I took. I was able to look at the old story with a kind of objectivity that was born out of knowing it wasn't real. It felt very real while it was happening, but in a single moment, everything could change. And it did. I thank The Nothing for destroying my false illusions.

This is why I want to share this story with you: It was "my work" that brought me to Japan. It was also quitting this work that gave me new life. The nothingness you feel is *not* nothing. It is everything within you calling to save yourself from the mistake of submitting to it. I value you and the life you chose. And if you are not 100% in love with it, I want you to know you can change it.

Before I went on the pilgrimage, I thought I had a great life. And I did. I am grateful for everything that has ever happened to me–the good and the bad–for it too is all an illusion. But it was like I was walking up the stairs of life, and before I knew it, the stairway turned into an escalator taking me to a destination that I did not want to go to. On the surface, it seemed great. I was an artist and I was getting incredible opportunities to make art that people thought was cool. Dancing with robots was something I could get a lot of funding for. It would get me prestige in my field for being innovative and daring. But my heart was not aligned with where I was headed. I couldn't look up and see the glorious adventure I was on because I wasn't willing to face what wasn't working. Only when I quit everything, did I find everything.

Now, if it sounds terrifying to quit it all in this moment, stick with me. I let it all go to find my path, but what I realized on that pilgrimage was that you don't necessarily have to. The structure of pilgrimage (and the many challenges and joys one can encounter) can be found in our daily lives. However, it can take something as epic as hitting rock bottom to shake us up. So I created a Virtual Pilgrimage, so that you can shake it up without breaking it up.

I don't think we have to find ourselves in a dumpster before we decide to change what isn't working. And when it comes to our work, well, that's our life. *Psychology Today* calculates that the average person spends 90,000 hours at work over their lifetime. We devote about half of our waking hours to our vocation. Shouldn't we make it something that feeds our soul? Shouldn't our work feel like love?

When we choose to treat our life's journey as a spiritual path, everything becomes sacred. Our work becomes our ministry. Our job is one of many platforms for us to express our truths. It doesn't matter if it is behind a desk or out in the fields, it is our opportunity to contribute to the world in a way that makes us sing. And it's possible to start now, wherever you may be.

The Virtual Pilgrimage is for you seekers who are tapped in enough to know that there must truly be more to life than this. You are right. There is so much more. And in this book, I will take you through the course that my pioneer pilgrims braved and came out victorious. By the end, you will be ready to phase out of your old life and into an adventure that saves the world from destruction.

I created this because I love you. I only commit to doing what I love now. And I can never turn back. If you want to join me in doing the same, I know we can take on the dark forces that threaten to destroy us. We can create a world built from our imaginations.

The Princess is asking you to give her a name, Bastian! Can you call it out? And can you accept the Call to Adventure??

The Hero's Inner Journey: Increased Awareness for Change
More people are going on pilgrimage than ever before to find their own DIY spiritual identity. In 2014, the United Nations held its first-ever

world conference of pilgrimage. They released a study there that found one-third of tourists are on a pilgrimage of one kind or another.

One of my pioneer virtual pilgrims, Carol, asked me early on why pilgrimage was important to me. It's a great question. Whether accidental (as in my case) or intentional (as in the best-case scenario), what is the motivation to do something so difficult?

Here's my answer after having gone on many: We go on pilgrimage to experience something deeper than the everyday, knowing there is more to life than what meets the eye. Pilgrims head out on the journey because they feel the spark of enlightenment within, the calling to go further on the path, to connect with holy sites in order to better connect with themselves and understand who they are in this world of illusion.

Pilgrimage allows us to follow a prescribed path that has been walked over thousands of years by countless masters, wise ones, and spirit seekers. By following in the footsteps of others, we actually find ourselves in the process. We deepen our connection with nature and are guided within and without to discover our true purpose and meaning of life.

Khandro Rinpoche, a prominent female Buddhist teacher, says, "One of the most beautiful ways of reflecting upon the karma that needs to be purified is pilgrimage. One of the very skillful ways and very beneficial ways and profound ways of acquiring merit is also through the pilgrimage." From a Buddhist perspective, you are doing yourself and others tremendous benefit through engaging in the act of pilgrimage.

On the quest for enlightenment and spiritual realization, a pilgrimage is an opportunity to experience all of the struggles, achievements, and ecstasies of life in a heightened form. The challenges—mental, physical, and spiritual—come very clearly and abundantly to life, as do the insights, revelations, and benefits of merit.

In short: pilgrimage is transformative. And it is transformation on a rapid scale.

We Can Be Heroes

I have been deeply practicing mind training and energy work ever since that fateful and life-changing pilgrimage in Japan in 2014. The two in combination are a powerful way to overcome obstacles and achieve tremendous results.

It may seem that a lot of the achievement on a pilgrimage comes from the grueling physicality of it all. However, it does not need to be so. Our minds create our physical reality. Our energy, our vibrations, are what cause our spirits to manifest into form. So we can start by working on that level, and it will have profound consequences in our daily lives. We can actually learn how to reprogram our subconscious minds and then consciously tap into an unlimited source of energy to achieve our dreams and heal our planet.

It's like Kundalini yoga: You get benefits from imagining doing the poses just as much as if you perform them physically. Numerous scientific studies have tested the effects of neurons that activate whether we are performing an action or observing it. If you do the necessary inner work of pilgrimage, you will also receive the spiritual and transformational benefits of pilgrimage.

There are as many types of pilgrimage as there are multiple spiritual paths, but there are common elements that lead to spiritual transformation. What I discovered is that the stages of pilgrimage mirror the structure of Joseph Campbell's Hero's Journey. Likewise, there is a corresponding Inner Journey, as Christopher Vogel clarified in *The Writer's Journey*. We use these structures in my program, The Hero's Way, to delve into the spiritual benefits, as well as to manifest meaningful work in the material realm. The course takes you on an inner journey that corresponds to the changes you wish to see in the world. It is a fun way to experience adventure without even leaving home. And the other part of the course works on creating a soulful business map so that you can move seamlessly from where you are to the work you are meant for. The end result is that you become a conscious creator of your experience, and you learn to make awesome money doing it.

A pilgrimage is about each person finding a spiritual connection of their own understanding. It need not be religious. Spirituality could mean being more connected to your intuition or open to guidance that feels divine. It could simply mean practicing patience, forgiveness, and happiness in your daily encounters. What is most important is the meaning it gives you to pursue the best life possible; when we are living in our bliss, we allow others to do the same.

Great Buddhist masters have been teaching for thousands of years that the world is not as "real" as it seems. Science, in particular quantum physics and neuroscience, are now verifying this to be true. We know that our minds create thought and turn it into substance. We know that through practice, we can transform the neural pathways in our brains. We know that all matter is made of energy. That means you, at your core, are energy. You are not solid. If you decide to go on this journey, you will be doing the work needed to change your life. Your beliefs about what is possible will change. The world around you will follow and you will be putting one foot in front of the other on the path to freedom.

"I just recently completed the pilgrimage and it was everything Sophia promised and more! Truly transformational!"
—Kim Woodcock

Chapter 2

FACE THE SHADOW,
FIND THE LIGHT

"The most regretful people on earth are those who felt the call to creative work, who felt their own creative power restive and uprising, and gave to it neither power nor time."

—**Mary Oliver**

Refusing the Call

It is at this early part of the pilgrimage that I like to visit the Shire of our furry-footed friends, the Hobbits. It is a lovely place, full of rolling green grassy knolls, plentiful foodstuffs, and joyous celebrations of the easy life. A sense of contentment sweeps over the minds of many here. Hobbits have family, love, and fireworks. It is easy to want for nothing in a place like the Shire.

But there is a war brewing. Much like The Nothing, there are dark forces at play. The war to rule the world is underway and the dark army will conquer everything in its path. They might not be felt in lands so far as the Shire, but even the Shire is not safe from such darkness.

Many of the Hobbits will turn a blind eye, seeking comfort over adventure. Some still, like one Hobbit hero, Bilbo Baggins, will resist when the wacky wizard comes to tell him of treasures and tricks him into throwing a party for dwarves. They disrupt his sense of order and he resists signing up to be their burglar to steal back their rightful treasures from the devious dragon Smaug. Despite his resistance, Bilbo sets out with this motley crew. And thank goodness! If not for Bilbo's humble heroics, he never would have returned with great treasure and the fulfillment of finding purpose and meaning. Most importantly, his nephew Frodo would never have inherited the ring that would end up saving them all.

This is the power of consciousness and choice. We are at a point where the world is so chaotic, we need to join all the tribes of Middle Earth to correct the course of great evil: We are either going to annihilate each other or the planet. You have a choice whether to spend the rest of your days drinking in merriment or pursuing the adventure that will bring you prosperity and peace.

It's easy to want to turn back now. You can close this book and never open it again. Or, like Bilbo mocked by a gang of dwarves, you can muster up all your indignance and set forth. Your adventure is to reclaim the treasure that has been stolen from you–your creative gold. When you get that back, you will have more abundance than you could have ever imagined. You will find new meaning in the adventure of your life. Most importantly, by simply committing to leave the Shire, you set forces in motion that will reverse the chaos and create a world of peace.

Will you sign a sacred contract with the universe to be the burglar on this journey–to steal back your life?

Your Hero's Journey: Fear / Resistance to Change

According to Bruce Feiler–host of PBS's excellent series *Sacred Journeys* and the bestseller *Walking the Bible*–for most of human history, meaning and identity were dictated to us. It came from our parents, community, society, geographical location, and any number of influences. Now we have a choice–who we want to be with, what religion we want to study, what work we want to do, where in the world we want to live–and ultimately, who we are and what we want to believe. It's easy to forget that just 100 years ago, we were much more limited in our capacity to choose our lives.

Right now, we are incredibly fortunate to live in a time where the world seems more interconnected than we have ever been able to perceive before. It's always been this way, but with current advances in technology and human consciousness, it is incredibly apparent. Recall the Butterfly Effect: Does the flap of a butterfly's wings in Brazil set off a tornado in Texas? A very small movement can cause a great change in a distant land. Because of the internet, telecommunications, travel, and media, we can see how directly our actions impact the world.

In fact, we don't just have an impact on the world. We actually create the world. Neuroscience details how our minds create a powerful current that creates our reality. Our thoughts create neurological patterns in our brains. These form the basis of emotional responses and these feelings create an even stronger signal. These form a feedback loop in our brains that becomes a state of being. We project this state outward and confirm it with our experience. Neurotransmitters also send these messages to our bodies that signal different glands in the body to make hormones. We can literally change our thoughts and change the physical reality of our bodies. In fact, the emergent field of epigenetics shows that even our genes are impacted by this process. Environmental signals, which include thoughts and emotions, directly affect our DNA expression. What we once thought was inherited and set in stone is actually malleable.

Your thoughts shape your world! So let's go back to claiming that treasure which is rightfully yours!

First, we have to face Smaug and solve the riddles needed to bring the money home. Let's enter that cave and see what's inside.

For example, let's say you have a pattern of fear programmed around money. You are afraid it won't be there when you need it, that you never have enough, or that you don't deserve it. Your thoughts will constantly be reinforcing the exact pattern that you fear, creating neurological pathways that send these signals to your body. Thus, from a subconscious level, you will be acting as if you do not have money or that you can't get it. This only reinforces the false thoughts that originate in your mind. But as we discussed, everything from your thoughts to your genetic make-up are malleable. They are not a hard truth. But unless you shine a light on these false beliefs, they will rule your world subconsciously.

So here's what will happen once you decide to change this patterning, once you decide to set foot on an epic journey that will forever change your life. You consciously know that you are doing what is best for your happiness so that you can better serve the world. (Otherwise, I think you would have put down this guide after reading the intro.) However, your subconscious mind—where all of your hidden fears, shadows, and negative thinking reside—will jump into alarm mode. Fear causes your animal instincts of fight, flight, freeze to activate when it encounters something new that challenges its deep beliefs and patterning. To the subconscious mind, new = scary. So it *will* try and stop you. The subconscious mind (we could also call this part "ego" or "small self") will come up with all kinds of excuses to try and convince you that you should turn back. It will tell you all kinds of things like:

- "You can't change your life *now*…you're already 42 years old!"
- "You were *born* this way. You inherited your personality from your mother. Everyone has always said so. People don't change."

- (No matter what age you are), "You're too old!"
- "What are you going to do for work? How can you possibly make a living by being a creative person in a world that doesn't support that?"
- "You need to pay your bills. And what if your car needs repairs again? You can't spend money on something you don't know will work."
- "This is some spiritual malarkey. You don't even believe in God or that there is a power you can't see that will help you. *Pssht.* Bullshit. Quit now and don't waste your time."
- "You have that bad back, remember? You get migraines once a month. You're too tired to go on a big journey. It doesn't matter if it's real or virtual."
- And so on.

Remember—our thoughts create our reality. The subconscious mind is a function of the mind after all. And because our subconscious minds have gone unchecked for so long, they have been powerfully co-creating a world we don't actually want. Take a minute to reflect on your day: how many moments are you actually aware of how you are creating what you see? For most of us, we spend the vast majority of our day overtaken by Monkey Mind chatter, that almost incessant voice inside that is planning, having fake conversations with people that aren't there, worrying about the future or dwelling on a past that no longer applies. It is really useful to log it for yourself. Think about today: Did you spend a few seconds outside of the Monkey Cage? A few minutes? Some days go by and you may not have even escaped at all.

And that's okay. Like I said, most of the world is right there with you. But you have a choice to change those numbers and spend an increasing amount of time resting in your presence and creating your present moment. I'll get to that in a bit.

Right now, however, your subconscious is likely freaking out because it can sense you are engaging with change. Besides all the crazy things it will try to convince you of, it will also create circumstances meant to stop you when you don't listen. For example:

- You might get sick and feel unfit for the task ahead.
- Some huge financial cost will come up sending a message that you can't afford to think of anything other than the job you already have.
- All of a sudden, you are bombarded with a new project at work and you have *no time* to pick up a book and read, let alone take a course or take time for healing and self-care.
- Your cat will die.
- Your sister will start a fight with you over nothing.
- Your partner will threaten to leave you.

All of these are very scary. And your subconscious will use these and countless other creative manifestations to attempt to derail you from your mission. But this is *your* path. This is *your* life. If you want to take back the reins, you must decide to do it. You must be all in, and know that things *will* come up. You will be setting off forces that have been messing up your life, insidiously covering it with a murky film so that you stay trapped below the surface of your beauty. Your ego-mind wants you to stay trapped in the dark and will continue to keep you there unless you choose to see a way out. How long can you live under wraps before you suffocate?

To deny your creative potential means that you are not truly living. Finding your freedom means taking a stand against the ego and saying, "I am going on this journey. You can stay here and wallow in your own misery, Ego. I leggo my Ego." When you do so, you join powers with forces far greater. They will help guide you where you want to go. But these forces need to know:

Are you IN???

If so, get ready to join the taskforce of Enlightenment Incorporated. *With our powers combined, we form: Captain Planet!* Better yet, we are like Captain Universe.

If you're in, get ready for a new world of adventure. You'll find a whole team of heroes, past and present, real and totally unreal, who are on your side and ready to save the world.

All you have to do is pack your bag. I already got you a ticket. I say, let's take a permanent vacation from ego-brain and start living in Universe Land.

What do you say?

"Sophia's Virtual Pilgrimage was a rejuvenating and engaging gift at this time of my life. I am startled by the impact working with her and allowing her to guide me has had on me. Her course opens and releases creative energy in the most loving yet direct way possible. Do it."

—Carol Rosenfeld

Chapter 3

YOU ALREADY HAVE
EVERYTHING YOU NEED TO FLY

"From the outer world the senses carry images to mind, which do not become myth, however, until they're transformed by fusion with accordant insights, awakened as imagination from the inner world of the body."

—Joseph Campbell

Meeting the Mentor

In *Alice's Adventures in Wonderland*, we begin with the mundane. Alice is bored and drowsy, listening to her sister read from a book with no pictures or conversations. So she takes the story into her own hands by chasing a White Rabbit down a rabbit hole and taking on a whole new adventure. In this "fantasy land," she meets all kinds of odd characters and has exciting encounters, a direct departure from her usual world. However, the characters in the book oddly resemble those in real life. And even in the book's ending, Alice at last awakens–not to a swarm of cards chopping off her head, but to her sister clearing fallen leaves off her face.

What is the story you choose? Can you take what you're doing now and make it mythic?

One way to improve the stories you live is to immerse yourself in stories that inspire you. Since we're embarking on a pilgrimage, what will you bring with you for entertainment?

I, for one, pick really specific reading materials and writing assignments to indulge in while traveling. I am also a huge sucker for in-flight movies. Put on anything Pixar so I can cry my eyeballs out or insane action flicks to suck me into an epic journey, and I can fly for days. Take a moment, close your eyes, and think about the kinds of things you want to be reading, watching, imagining.

Doesn't it already feel good to get out of the office, soak in some inspiration, and dream of where you'll land???

Now, let's not get confused here. You are not going to suntan on the beaches of the Bahamas. *We're on a Pilgrimage*, remember? It will be full of wild adventures, and in the end, you will earn your well-deserved rest on the beach. But if you're on this airplane with me, then you've said, "Yes! I packed my bags, and I am on a journey to reach new levels of clarity, find meaningful work, and step into a happier life!"

As such, you will be required to show up for yourself and the journey daily. The amount of time you commit is up to you, and you will receive the most benefits for this if you can dive in with an open heart and a genuine desire to go on a journey that has positive merit for yourself and others. But I want to make sure you're prepared and understand exactly what you'll need to reap the benefits.

So let's revisit what movies you'll watch and books you'll read on this particular journey. I like to align my reading material with the specifics of a journey. For example, I read *Lagoon* by Nnedi Okorafor while I was creating art in West Africa. It's a mystical modern alien tale set in Nigeria. I was obviously the alien in my real-life story. I read *A Tale for The Time Being* by Ruth Ozeki while I went on Pilgrimage in Shikoku, Japan. A young Japanese girl finds her spiritual path and discovers mysteries of reality through her connection with her paradox-embracing grandmother, a Buddhist nun. Another woman finds the girl's journal and saves herself through her dedication to knowing how the story ends. I was every character in that one. I align my chosen stories with the life I choose to live.

Since this journey is a virtual one, you will be bringing the stories that you carry in your mind. (I'll also provide a reading list at the end of this book for further aligned reading material.) You also get to choose new stories that you can live up to.

One common spiritual tenet is that all the wisdom you seek is within. In Kundalini, yogis bow and say "Sat Nam" at the end of a practice. This roughly translates to "truth identified," honoring the truth that is within ourselves and in all beings. There's a wonderful documentary currently on Netflix called *Kumaré*, which reveals how our entire lives are merely a performance. By posing as an Indian guru, Vikram Ghandi tenderly teaches his students how the real guru lies within.

What are some of your favorite novels, movies, and stories? Does the main character meet a mentor in them? Make a list and note who the mentors are. How did they reveal the hero already existing inside their student?

One of my all-time favorites is Star Wars. Yoda's whole jam is to prove to Luke that he always had the Force within. Luke learns from his inner knowing by confronting his shadows in the wilderness. In his mind, he meets Darth Vader and slays him, only to reveal that he is the face under the mask.

You, too, have this power within you. You, too, have the wisdom needed to find your way.

Your Hero's Journey: Overcoming Fear

Let's look at the story you've brought along with you for this journey. Take 10 minutes and freewrite in your journal. Put the pen to paper and write without thinking or stopping. Answer the question: Who am I?

What is your current life story? Where do you live? What is your work? What do you love to do? What are some things that drive you crazy? What are your goals and dreams? What constitutes who you are? Write down whatever comes up for you.

One of the best ways to access the wisdom of your inner guru is to get clear on three things:

1. Motivations
2. Intentions
3. Aspirations

So let's get clear!

Do yourself a favor and turn to yourself like a good friend. Take to your journal and spend another 10 minutes to write down: Why am I here? As in, what caused you to pick up this book in the first place? What was your *motivation* for coming on this journey within its pages? Why are you doing this and what do you hope to achieve?

Intentions:

When I was in Shikoku, I made some specific intentions for the pilgrimage because of what was happening in my life. So, for example, because I had been letting go and breaking habits that I had really been tied to in NY, I made these intentions:

- I would stop pushing myself to achieve, to only go as far as I could go without stressing about it.
- I would figure out what my true pace was by going slower.
- When I met up with another pilgrim, I would go with their pace so I didn't get stuck with my own ideas of time.

So what intentions can you set about how you will show up for yourself and others in this pilgrimage?

1. "If money was no concern and you had all the time and money in the world, what would you do?" Make a list.
2. Ask yourself, "How am I best suited to serve humanity?"
3. Do you have spiritual beliefs? Were you raised in a particular religious tradition growing up? What are your beliefs now?
4. What is your intention for showing up today? What is your intention for this journey? (It could be a specific goal or simply to be more present in your life. Whatever it may be, make it clear and state it for yourself as you wake up each day. Allow it to change and evolve as you continue on.)

I want to address the topic of spirituality for a moment and reiterate: *it does not matter what or who you believe in (if anything at all!)* You can call the forces-that-be God, Universe, Buddha, the Divine, Vortex, Nature, the Quantum Field, Allah, or Emptiness. True spirituality is not dogma; it is simply a path to reveal that you are a manifestation of this force. You are your own inner guru and you have the ability to achieve deep and abiding wisdom.

Throughout this book, I will pull from various spiritual teachings in order to illuminate this point. Though I deeply study Tibetan Buddhism now, I was raised Christian, and really dig a lot about Taoism, Shamanic Studies, Zen Buddhism, Hinduism, and the metaphysical text, *A Course in Miracles*. In fact, I love all spiritual disciplines. I believe that what ties them all together is love.

Meeting My Mentor

When I went on that accidental pilgrimage in 2014, I had barely a hint of what Buddhism was. I had studied Christianity for the major part of my early life, and then decided to pursue a personal path.

After completing the Shikoku Pilgrimage, I began delving deeper into Vajrayana Buddhism because I find it magical and illuminating. However, Buddhism is *not* dogma. It is simply a way to examine one's existence and apply it to the world with compassion. The Buddha said to examine the teachings as a goldsmith would examine gold. If you can come up with a better explanation of how things work, Buddhism will adapt. (Most people find that teachings really do apply quite well.) I personally love a spiritual discipline built on the foundation of questioning and experimentation. However, it is one tool among many to reach spiritual realization.

The only thing you need to go on this pilgrimage is yourself.

Keeping in mind your intentions and destination will get you where you want to go. Knowing what drives you allows you to steer. Having a map leads you to the treasure. Your mind and your intuition are your compass to return you to your course, available to you at all times. Part of the journey is finding unexpected adventure that you never could have planned. Oh, the stories you'll tell about *how* you actually got here.

There are three keys to unlock new pathways on your adventure. They are: Being, Doing, Having. In order to get to your final destination—The You You Aspire to Be—we have to go in reverse order.

So get out that pen and paper again! What do you aspire to *have*?

- What do you want to *have* happen in your life?
- What job would you *have* if you could do anything?
- What else would you *have* if you were doing what you love?

Allow yourself to dream on the page of the wonders you will encounter in this new story!

Here's the best news: Because this journey starts in your mind, you already have everything you need to complete it.

It's really great that you packed that extra sweater. There will be many chilly nights where you must face the feelings that arise. However, the best thing that you brought with you is your big, beautiful mind. Let's put that to use to entertain us on this airplane. It will be the inspirational source to get us to where we need to go.

So back to our thoughts for a moment. We have many, many thoughts whose signals create hundreds of trillions of neural pathways in our brains. What we do to make sense of our world is put them all together and create narrative threads between them. Start with the question above: Who am I? This is the main character of our story. It's you! Congratulations, you have the starring role of the greatest movie you will ever watch.

> "A Course in Miracles *teaches us that projection is perception. This means that whatever stories you're projecting in your mind are what you're perceiving in your life.*"
> —**Gabrielle Bernstein**, *The Universe Has Your Back*

We take these stories–pieced together from our memories, thoughts, and experiences–and play them on the projection screen of our life. Are you paying close attention to your story? Are you watching the horror movie playing on the screen and screaming at the busty actress running from the killer, "For the love of God, do not lock yourself upstairs where you can't escape!!!" We repeat the same patterns over and over again, frustrated by what we see materialize around us. We are that actress who's not really thinking clearly when we are operating out of fear. Remember Ego that we left behind on this journey? Ego only wanted to keep us safe, but did not truly know what was best for us. He's not here hogging the remote now. You can change the channel on this in-flight film and watch *The Princess Bride* instead of *Texas Chainsaw Massacre*. Your intentions and clear direction will allow you to watch an inspiring film aligned with this particular journey.

There's a time and place for scary movies, and we'll watch some later. For now, recline your seat back and relax because we are about to cross the threshold into Special World. It is here where you will find out what you are really made of.

Chapter 4

BUT DO MAKE SURE YOU BRING YOUR SPECIAL WEAPONS

"Those who don't believe in magic will never find it."
—**Roald Dahl**

Crossing the Threshold

You have left the Shire and are entering Middle Earth to face the fires of Mordor. There will be all kinds of scary creatures and unforgiving demons waiting to derail you from your mission. If you want to restore peace and justice to the land, you will be tried. You'll need some new tools. We'll pick these up at the duty-free store when we land in Special World.

In the meantime, are you enjoying flying?

As a little kid, I loved it. Growing up, our family didn't have a lot of money. So the first vacation we ever took was when I was 8. We went to Disney World in Orlando, Florida. I remember getting up from my seat every 20 minutes or so, making up all kinds of excuses so I could feel my scrawny little body navigating the aisles while being carried through the air. I was taking flight. I was filled with possibility.

I still love it now. I work a lot, so for me, it's time to rest, watch movies, listen to music, read, sleep, get some writing done. I feel taken care of and contained in one space. There's nowhere for me to go and distract myself with Doing.

Here's the second key to unlocking adventure pathways: Doing.

Writing Opportunity! Take 10 minutes to freewrite in your journal:

- What do you *do*?
- What do you do for work? Fun?
- Are you very active?

I'm an over-doer. One of my old habits is that I am a workaholic. That's my story. Are you similar? Or do you hang out on the other end of the spectrum? Are you at peace doing absolutely nothing? Vegging out on the couch watching Netflix series after series for days on end is your jam? Or maybe you're somewhere in between? Can you assess how you do?

Let's also make sure not to judge ourselves for whatever comes up. You are *doing* great. Everything we look at is part of an old movie, habits that we've acquired throughout our lives. They are malleable, remember. We'll get to that really soon, but it's important to look and see what's there first. And here's one way to do that, which encompasses both doing and not doing. Did you guess it?

It's meditation!!!

Okay, now notice what your reaction was to that. Is it a relief that there are simple practices that can help you tap into your personal power? Or does it fill you with dread to imagine yourself sitting still? Perhaps you have tried mediation and "it didn't work for you." This is common. Are you open to trying again?

Because, my dear hero-in-training, you are crossing over into Special World. Meditation is your secret weapon that will allow you to slay the demons, dragons, and dark forces that would seek to stop you. We can start practicing now to prepare.

In Japanese Zen Buddhism, one of the famous practices is called Zen Mind, Beginner's Mind. This means approaching everything as if it were the first time you were doing it. It is an incredibly useful practice, considering that you never actually do the same thing twice. You are a different person in every moment on a cellular level. Our shed skin cells cover the furniture, but we don't usually notice. We are changing constantly. Even something as simple as brushing your teeth is different every day. The time of day is different, the weather conditions, what is happening in your life at that moment—all of it colors how you brush your teeth. So let's get really meta and approach meditation in this moment as if it's the first time we've ever done it. Whether you tried it and didn't like it, or if you are a serious practitioner, it's different right now, in this moment. Let's begin again. Zen Mind, Beginner's Mind.

So how is meditation going to be your secret weapon on this journey?

What meditation does is quiet all the noise and allow you to tap into what is truly meaningful to you. When something happens (and something is happening all the time), we tend to have a reaction to it. We trigger a system of instantaneous thoughts and emotions. This happens without us knowing and we behave accordingly. We enter into a state of being that causes us to face the same scenarios time and again. Meditation slows down the process, so we can actually see it happening. With consistent practice, we are no longer in a state of constant reaction, but we can more consciously make choices about how we want to respond.

On my first trip to India, I was with my collaborator Jayme. We were on a Compassionate Social Action mission, and went to visit school children in one of the biggest slums in Delhi. As we were walking down the dirt road, a man was walking directly toward us. He was dressed all in white, except his white clothes were covered almost entirely in blood. It is possible he was also holding a knife. I had been seriously practicing meditation for many years leading up to that moment. If it were years before, I probably would have frozen in fear or ran away or screamed... or something! Instead, I remember focusing consciously on my breath and looking directly at him. Feeling my breath. Feeling my breath. In moments, Jayme exclaimed, "I don't think you're seeing what I'm seeing!" I nodded my head and said, "Oh, I'm seeing it... I'm just not reacting."

That clear moment revealed how meditation changes what we see. Turns out, the Indian man was just doing his job, which happens to be murdering chickens. I chose in that instant not to be a chicken.

When things happen to you, what matters is how your mind perceives it. We've all been through various types and levels of trauma. It really does matter how we perceive it. Take Viktor Frankl, for example. Frankl was an Austrian neurologist and psychiatrist who suffered horrific experiences as a concentration camp inmate during WWII. These experiences led him to discover the importance of finding meaning in all of existence, even the most brutal and dehumanizing.

There are many kinds of meditation, including sitting meditation, walking meditation, mantra, silent, loving-kindness, active, and mindfulness meditation. The point is not to sit still and get rid of your thoughts (which is impossible and would turn you into a zombie).

The point is to increase your awareness of the inner workings of your own mind.

So are you willing to meditate and see how it changes your perception of the world?

Here are two ways to look at it, from the practical to the fantastical:

1. If life feels difficult for you, and it's hard to get your butt on a cushion, it might motivate you to know that meditation has tremendous benefits that will relieve pain and promote wellbeing. Meditation significantly lowers the levels of stress hormones, such as adrenaline and cortisol. It helps calm the mind, which helps induce sleep. Meditation creates space for clarity and creativity, which are keys to performing better at work and beyond.

Richard Davidson is a neuroscientist who has done numerous studies on serious meditation practitioners. He claims that 8 minutes is the minimum needed to create definite changes in the brain. Eight minutes is not a lot when there are 24 hours in a day! I know you may *feel* like you don't have any time (and I am about to bust that myth in the coming chapters), but the act of meditating actually opens up *more* time for you. It creates a spaciousness in the mind that allows you to perceive time differently. Thus, it actually creates more time. You don't have time *not* to meditate! So if one of your excuses is that you don't have time, then you need it the most. And if you do have time, then there is no excuse.

Even one minute will create a gap in the constant stream of Monkey Mind chatter and provide you with great relief–if you let it.

So let's do it! Because here's the most fantastical part:

2. Mediation opens up portals to realms that we otherwise can't perceive.

My Hero's Journey: Committing to Change

Here's an example from my life: On my Virtual Pilgrimage, I performed weekly Sacred Site Energy Healings for the pilgrims. Energy healings are super important while doing this life-changing work because they aid in clearing out blocked energy from the chakras and realigning each person to their unique energy frequency to help achieve their goals. They are a meditation unto themselves. On the last pilgrimage, I was in retreat at the Sangdo Palri Temple and getting up at the crack of dawn to be up at the top of the mountain for the first sitting session. So I had to get up *even* earlier to do the healing for my pilgrims.

Upon waking up is one of the best times to meditate. Our brain states are moving from Alpha to Beta states, where we can transition beyond the conscious mind and enter the subconscious mind. In this zone, we can change destructive habits, emotional reactions, behaviors, and unconscious states of being. This time, I peeled myself out of bed, from the warm house where I yearned to make tea and get ready for my day, to head out into the frosty mountains to do the energy healing. While I was out there, something magical happened. I can only say that I discovered a portal in the woods that I crossed through. Clear as day, all my pilgrims were there. We did a ritual crossing over a bridge to begin the journey together and I emerged wondering: *WTF just happened back there? No one else was there, but they were THERE.*

Afterwards, there was a giant shift in my connection to the pilgrims. Julia experienced guidance from her deceased grandmother during the healing. Kim told me that she journeyed to a healing cave where she can bathe in healing light and warmth. The Sacred Site healings had miraculous effects and turned out to be one of the most impactful parts of the program.

This may sound crazy, and I accept that. But magic and miracles begin to happen when you transcend the conventional mind and its unnecessary chatter. This is why a continued meditation practice works wonders. Time and time again, I remember to peel myself away from the computer, everyday worries, and things I feel I should be doing to do this simple act of transcendence.

Giving yourself the gift of time is one of the most important things you could do. I delve deeply into developing a meditation practice with my Virtual Pilgrims, but you can start practicing right now in whatever way feels right for you. Feel free to Choose Your Own Adventure, but do choose to do what is good for you.

When you go within, you find an unlimited source of courage and wisdom. It is good for you to carry this with you as we leave Ordinary World and move further into Special World.

Chapter 5

YOUR ENEMIES AWAIT;
SO DO YOUR ALLIES

"We have met the enemy and he is us."
—**Walt Kelly**, *Pogo~*

Tests, Allies, Enemies

Good morning, this is your flight captain speaking. Looks like we've reached our final destination right on time.

Star Date: 13-12.9

Local time: 11:11AM

Local Temperature: 69 degrees

We hope you've enjoyed your flight. It was a pleasure flying the fantastical skies with you. Enjoy your stay in Special World and take care on the rest of your journey. We look forward to flying with you again soon.

Your Hero's Journey: Experimenting with New Conditions

Welcome to Special World, Hero! You are entering a new realm full of unfamiliar rules and values. It is time for you to test these conditions and you *will* be tested accordingly. I hope you've brought your stillness of mind. You've got a new job to do and a world to save.

You've gone from being Bruce Wayne–a tortured individual hiding behind his public persona–to the Dark Knight, ready to restore some sanity to this town (and slaughter some shadows so doing). Your job right now is to go into the depths of your own personal Batcave and look at the story that brought you here to this day. How you ended up here is exactly the path to your freedom. Get excited because if you are not working a job you love, it is exactly that job that will help you get where you want to be.

I'm going to share with you one of the secrets of Special World. Knowing this in advance will help you to battle your enemies and find your allies: In Special World, everything is an illusion. Once you face your fear, it dissipates. Embrace your destiny and it comes rushing toward you. In fact, this is the way in Ordinary World as well. Therefore, if you use Special World as training grounds for practicing your magic, you will be able to practice this upon your triumphant return.

So are you ready to restore peace to the universe??

Great—let's do it!

Remember how your thoughts create your reality? Here's more on that:

> *"What we focus on we create–be it good or bad. The stories we project on our internal movie screens become the experiences we perceive to be our realities. We spend our days collecting information*

and images to support our inner movies. We are in a constant state of focusing on certain images and filtering out others. In doing so, we are actively choosing the world we perceive."

—**Gabrielle Bernstein**, *The Universe Has Your Back*

Remember back in Ordinary World, how you were feeling stuck in work you weren't in love with? Our fear stories in our minds can keep us in freezer-mode, so that we are not headed in the direction of our dreams. All it takes is a shift in our thinking to set us back in motion. And our thoughts create this world. So let's look at the fear stories you've been spinning, so that we can pierce through the illusion and be done with them once and for all.

Neuroscientists have discovered something fascinating about our love of scary movies. Turns out, our brain reacts differently to a horror movie than to the "real thing" as induced in the laboratory. The conventions of the horror movie seem to tell the brain that this isn't real. We may describe the movie as scary, but our brain activity is actually much more similar to exhilaration than fear. This explains why they are so addictive. The combined feelings of anxiety, suspense, and excitement are accompanied by neural transmitters that generate a natural "high" in the brain, making us want more and more of the same mix of chemicals to give us that rush. (From learningtogo.info)

So what if we can look at the negative movies we are projecting on our lives and know that they are not real? Can we then live in a state of natural and healthy exhilaration?

Let's see!

What are you afraid of? Take 10 minutes and freewrite this one out. If I tell you that you can have the job of your dreams and live in abundance with joy and purpose, what comes up for you? Is it impossible or possible? What would stop you?

How would this relate to other people in your life?

There are other characters in this movie of your life, such as family members, friends, colleagues. There's an antagonist, such as a political leader or an entire taskforce of darkness. Who and what do you fear?

We want to identify these fears because they are the blocks that are preventing you from your freedom. The third key to living your spiritual and creative path is: Having, Doing, and *Being*. So how are we acting when in the face of fear? Who are we being?

Think about Batman: He is haunted by the murder of his parents at an early age by hooligans. So he spends his entire existence tracking them down and ridding the world of their wrong-doings. The way out is in. We must keep facing this darkness until it is eradicated. Batman knows this. If he were to give in to his own darkness, Gotham would fall. Instead, he seeks it out and restores the city to safety time and time again.

In these next few exercises, we'll go even further in and reveal some of your enemies. You'll unleash your superpowers so that you can hone the tools you already have within you to defeat them. So get out your trusty pen—this is one of your special weapons to figure out the old fear story and rewrite the one you want to be living.

1. What is your earliest memory as a child? (Our stories are formed before we turn 7 years old. Our earliest memory is often a key indicator of patterns we develop and reinforce throughout our lifetime.)

2. What happened the first time you remember "losing it" and getting really upset in your childhood? What was the inciting event or experience?

3. What have you always done extremely well, that you do not remember ever learning how to do? What do you believe your gifts are?

4. What are your interests and obsessions? Make a list.

5. Ask others what your three best qualities are. It may seem weird at first, but this gets really fun once you get used to it. Ask 20 – 30 people and find the threads between their answers. These are your superpowers!

Remember, your stories are how you choose to perceive the world. When we are living stuck in our fear stories, the world appears full of enemies. When we embrace the stories that have caused us to become the person we are today–the ones that guide us to who we want to be–the world conspires to aid us on our mission.

My Tests, Enemies, and Allies

When I was studying abroad in Florence, Italy, our apartment burned down. The fire trucks couldn't get down the narrow cobblestone street, so we had to watch as our lives burned before our eyes. Our professor said he hadn't seen a fire in Florence in the 50 years he'd lived there. No one really knew what to do. And the five of us young American college students had hugely varying reactions. One decided to pee while the apartment burst into flames because "she didn't know when she'd get to go again." Another gathered her passport and cash while the window exploded next to her. Others were filling buckets with water (which we were unaware does not actually extinguish an electrical fire). One was kicking car tires in despair. Another called her boyfriend back at home for moral support. There were any number of ways that event could be perceived. Who were we *being* to deal with crisis when it struck?

It turned out fine. We had to wear the same clothes for days. When we got back what didn't burn up, it smelled like smoked ham. But we all survived, and got an even better apartment in the end. Moreover, we learned to appreciate life in a whole new way.

If your house burns down, you could see it as losing everything you own or an opportunity to get that house you've always dreamed of. If you are out of work, you could see it as a loss of income or an opportunity to make up whatever work you want. How will you perceive the fear stories that have been running your life? Will you let them bring you down or will you put on your utility belt, jump in your Batmobile, and ride off to save Gotham?

Chapter 6

BUSTING THE MYTHS
OF ORDINARY WORLD

"You have no power over me!"
—**Sarah Williams**, *Labyrinth*

Approaching the Inmost Cave

You are at the pinnacle!

Now that we've looked at the illusion of fear and the world of chaos that it creates, you are approaching the Inmost Cave on your Hero's Journey. Your team of comrades is with you–the brave, strong, and courageous ones who will continue to slice through their fears with the swords of mindfulness! Get prepared to challenge your false beliefs about this world and prepare for major change!

I'm with you! And now to prepare for you greatest challenge yet, I present you with a golden elixir, a truth serum to wash away the Three Major Myths of Ordinary World: Not Enough Time, Not Enough Money, and Not Enough Energy. This is an exciting moment because, if you ingest this, you will become infinite.

In Special World, anything is possible. In fact, Special World is really the realm of magical possibility that has the potential to manifest in Ordinary World. But we have to go *way* out there to realize exactly what we have here.

A perfect illustration of the illusions of our world is the movie *Labyrinth*. David Bowie and Jim Henson's brilliance aside, it is a testament to the world we create with our fantasies.

Sarah Williams is in despair over the frustrations of daily life and wishes her baby brother Toby to be taken away by the Goblin King. Her wish is granted. Upon realizing the power of her intentions, she attempts to rescue him before he too is transformed into a goblin. To do so, she must solve a labyrinth in a seemingly impossible amount of time to get him back.

The labyrinth is constantly shifting and throwing Sarah for a loop. But when Sarah turns her mind to love and creative solutions, myriad allies show up to help her solve the puzzle. Hoggle, the worm, Ludo, and Sir Didymus, among others, appear to guide her where she needs to be. In the end, Sarah rescues Toby, and her allies show up in her bedroom. They profess their loyalty and that they will always be there, "Should you need us." (We always do find the support we need when we need it most.) Then, they proceed to have a dance party in celebration.

We have to push our own boundaries if we are going to expand. If we want to break out of the habits that have trapped us into cubicles and behind bars (both slinging drinks and in the confines of our own personal prisons), we have got to go where we haven't before. This is the big magic of creativity. Since the beginning of humankind, we have been creators and makers. We make stuff up, and then it becomes real. We get to go there in our minds and make it real. The best examples come from science fiction. Creative writers dreamt of driverless cars and dancing robots. Now they exist. Steve Jobs dreamt that one day every home would have a personal computer. We are pretty darn close to that today. The teleporter in Star Trek could convert a person into an energy pattern, "beam" it to a target and reconvert it into matter. We are going to do that now. We are going to take our own expeditions, our life's work, and reconfigure it so that we can create a new world.

Look, all we really have is the present moment. And that moment is actually devoid of the human conceptual notions of time, space, and matter. You can't capture the present moment because once you think about it, it's already a new one. Meditation is critical to entering into the present. We can slip into the realm of creative possibility when we let go of linear time, "when we are no longer fixated on memories of the past and expectations of a same as usual future." Dr. Joe Dispenza chronicles this incredibly well in his book *Breaking the Habit of Being Yourself*. He talks about overcoming the body, environment, and time so that you can close the gap between who you are and who you want to become. These are similar to the gateways I use: Time, Money, and Energy. Right now, at least one of these is stopping you from fulfilling your grand potential. Breaking through these blocks will allow you to be the hero you already are; it will allow you to consciously transcend the conventional world and collaborate with the quantum field.

But let's say you're not at a point yet where you can wash away the material world by slipping into the quantum field. There's still this whole life you have to deal with–your boss is stressing you out; your partner is needy; you wish you had more money to buy things that would make you feel healthier and happier; you are exhausted thinking about anything other than crashing on the couch after work and watching *America's Got Talent.*

Let's put this in perspective: None of that stuff really matters. In truth, it only exists because you choose for it to be so. You can choose again. You can focus on this present moment and how it's truly all you have.

Approaching My Inmost Cave

My African Pilgrimage showed me how important it is to tap into the Now. In Diébougou, Burkina Faso, there are funerals every week. People put their lives on hold every week so that they can attend to the sick or honor the dead. Death and sickness are the norm. I got a fever every few days. That's normal. Nadi, my host family sister, told me her best friend died in Gawa. Ahmed, our lighting and sound technician, told me he couldn't promise to get a black-out switch because a family member had passed away. (Despite this, he did travel out of town to get the switch.) Mishibelle, Yuko's host family sister, has a baby who can't walk. She had twins but the sibling died at birth. They are happy to have the one child despite the disability.

Life (and death) feel more intense in Africa. The reminders of impermanence returned me to the question: What is my purpose?

We never know when we are going to go. It doesn't matter what age we are—infant, university student, elder—when it's our time, we go. It is a reminder to live our lives in the best way possible. That means living with purpose, not wasting our precious time on this glorious planet.

Your Hero's Journey: Preparing for Major Change

One issue that I hear a lot is a kind of habituated apathy: "What if I don't know what my purpose is?" It's a depressing thought. So we could use it as an excuse, and stop looking. But our purpose is always changing, just as we are. So instead of looking for this amorphous thing called "purpose," we can always, in every moment, live our lives *with* purpose.

What does this mean? Well, we start by getting real with ourselves and researching our lives. Start right now with the now. There is truly no other time.

Ask yourself these two questions:

1. What's life about?

Some will say "fun," others will say "helping others." These two people live in completely different worlds with different perspectives, values, and goals. One isn't necessarily better than another. But to know your priorities is to know how you want to live.

For me, in this moment, life is about creating connections, being of service, helping enlighten our world.

What is life about for you?

2. And super importantly: How do you most want to *feel* in your life?

This exercise is from Danielle LaPorte's *Desire Map*. Honing down on your Core Desired Feelings–3-5 words that articulate how you most want to feel–can be your guidepost to living in ways that are fully aligned with the core of your being. Making a To Do List based off of how you want to feel changes the list entirely. By acting in accordance with our feelings, we generate an undeniable energy that brings back more of what we want to feel. Energy is contagious. By defining ours, we can decide if it's going to be a contagious illness or an energy generator of unlimited power.

When you wake up every day, how do you want to feel? When you die, you want to be able to say "I was _____."

We Can Be Heroes

There is a misconception in Buddhism that we are to renounce our desires and live a life of asceticism. In fact, Shakyamuni Buddha renounced the material world only to return to it, knowing that asceticism is not the true path to enlightenment. We can transcend this world only by fully understanding it, and this includes our desires.

Our desires are the most powerful positive forces that drive us to act. Too often they are suppressed. So do everyone a favor and get in touch with yours. Set them free. Love them. And let them lead you to your dreams.

When we are guided by love, even the most impossible labyrinths can be solved.

My Journey Continues

Our Inmost Cave is filled with the fears, shadows, and dangers that we need to conquer in order to emerge victorious. Often, when people experience resistance and discomfort, we try to get away from it ASAP. We want to feel good all the time and when we don't, we'll try all kinds of strategies to feel better fast. We either grasp for things to make us feel better or reject what makes us feel bad. Addiction is an extreme form; habitual behaviors develop as subtle means to feel like we're in control.

But what if every obstacle is an opportunity for growth—a kind of obstacle course to train you for winning the gold medal called your Life's Purpose?

It helps me to think about challenge as growth when I am in times of extreme duress. Reframing obstacles as opportunities in disguise helps me to have the strength to meet them. I know that when conditions change (which they always do), I will have leveled up and be ever closer to living my dreams.

In India, it's not particularly easy to stay healthy. Since I went from India to Africa, I wasn't entirely healthy for months. It's challenging to travel when your body is freaking out. And then, meet the African toilet. It's a hole in clay ground with a water pitcher to wash off (sometimes). Even the Asian/Indian ground toilet tends to have some porcelain to drop it into. Fancy in comparison. They do not even sell toilet paper in Burkina as far as I could see.

And then, get your period on the first full day when you have to take a searing hot bus ride crammed full of people that only stops for the African toilet once.

In fact, meet the entire situation in Africa, where I was never entirely sure what was happening at any given moment. Basically, everything was an obstacle.

Here are a few more:

1. I didn't speak French (or any of the 60 native languages), so I was never really sure where I was going or what I was doing or when or how or anything. I only had Miyu and Yuko who spoke English well, and they are Japanese. There were a bunch of other Japanese people in Burkina, so they were always speaking in Japanese. That would have been fine for me (I was quite enjoying this Japanese refresher and could understand a lot by what I gleaned from their conversations), but the cacophony of languages made everything sound a bit like Charlie Brown's teacher. If people were speaking only French or only Japanese, I could have focused on learning one or the other. But I was learning both simultaneously, and my brain hurt. So I was *fatigué* most of the time.

"This is real Africa."
—Miyu

2. Burkina Faso was different than anywhere I've ever been (though some things bear a striking resemblance to India).

I was staying with a host family. Miyu placed me with Marcus because he said he speaks English "no problem." He did not. And being in any new foreign country requires figuring out the culture. So, for example, when they gave me my bed and there was no sheet on it, was that a cultural thing? Or did he just forget? And how should I ask about that? Or was I supposed to just accept that there was no sheet?

I didn't really know who anyone was, i.e., whether the people who worked at home were family or hired help. There were always people around and I wasn't even sure most times who lived in that small house.

And if it's a cultural thing not to use sheets on the mattress, then why, when I snuck a peek in the other bedrooms, did I see that they had sheets?

And how the heck do I use the toilet water without spilling it all in my shoe?!?

The eating with hands thing goes to a whole new level in Burkina, and I had to get over my fear of germs (everyone wanted to shake or hold hands). I had to get over wanting to remain clean for more than an hour after bathing. I was dirty all the time and imbibing food items I would not normally eat. I had to accept this in order to find peace there.

So I approached Sylvie (who I thought was Marcus' sister but was always cooking and cleaning and being treated differently than the other girls). I asked Sylvie about the sheet situation in mangled English-French weirdness. She seemed to understand, but did not actually know if there were sheets. In mangled English-French she told me I had to ask Marcus, who never seemed to be home. And his wife left the day I arrived to go see her father who was sick. So a lot of times, I actually found myself at home alone with the four young girls of the house. I at least bonded with them on some small level, especially "DouDou," who was three years old and loved for me to watch her dance and fall over repeatedly on the floor.

And speaking of dancing and falling on the floor, that was what we were doing in Yuko's Butoh dance workshop on dubious floor quality. Our rehearsal space consisted of shattered flooring that resembled my own mind.

3. Upon arriving, Miyu told me I had to teach a 5-day theater workshop. This was strikingly different from "Come and we'll explore together. You can do whatever you want."

After the soggy, 5-hour bus ride, we had a meeting with the committee for the NyamaNyama Festival. Miyu deemed it necessary to have something to show for the festival. So even though I wanted to be there more for research, I acquiesced. "Okay, cool. I don't feel great and I haven't really taught (let alone created) theater in years, but sure, I'll teach a theater workshop."

And then, if that wasn't enough to force me to deal with, I was asked to collaboratively teach the workshop with an African man from the main city of Ougadougou. At first I was excited about sharing the load. I thought it would be a relief and a joy.

And then...

Well, there is so much I could say about that situation. In a nutshell, he was more interested in doing what he wanted to do–directing all the actors instead of collaborating or being open to just about anything from anyone. I was being all "patience practice" with him, but Miyu was super annoyed up front. As the translator, she felt like she may have spoken too harshly or out of her own frustration with him. She made it right, but other people that witnessed him were turned off as well. I felt like his ego was big, his energy heavy, and it made things difficult. It was not fun.

So I gave up on making a piece with them or fulfilling Miyu's wish that I open up the actors' minds to more theater than the two types here:

1. very conventional straight theater
2. "theater" with a social message (which is just people giving a lecture)

At one point, I muttered the words, "I am dying inside." Everything in me knew that I could work with those beautiful actors to make something extraordinary.

Herein lies a great artistic challenge. And one of life: how to challenge the status quo while being challenged by it.

The obstacles we perceive are merely shadows we haven't fully shined the light on. We must look at them if we are to transform. If we succumb to the Victim Archetype and cast someone in our drama as the Villain, we will always fail. Our real power comes from taking personal responsibility. Some things in life are not for us to decide, but we can decide what to do with what we've been given. If the world and all of its many distractions feels chaotic or misaligned, we can find the interior pattern that is causing the challenge. We have more control than we often perceive. We have the power to change our perception.

Here are my observations gleaned from my own obstacles:

1. I see health crises as healing crises now, like purifications. Afterwards, I feel stronger, like developing immunity.

2. I learn Japanese and French best by relaxing my mind and simply being present. When I keep my mind open and flexible, taking in all sound and not getting tight around what I don't understand, I can communicate. Not being able to rely on language forces me to actually be a *better*

communicator. And it does an awesome job humbling the ego. (Bonus Buddhism points.)

3. I am learning so much. It wasn't always clear at the time what the lessons were. It is through reflection that we discover meaning. I know that learning can be really hard. It can feel painful, like strength training. The muscles get fatigued, but if you don't keep stretching them and breathing through the tightness, you'll either get injured or there won't be progress.

   I also know that we learn a lot by making mistakes, by learning what not to do. Getting over shame and embarrassment is big. I learned this because while everything in Africa felt confusing, it all turned out to be fine.

4. Living in Africa and India made me much more tolerant. Wow, do I appreciate life in the U.S.! I wasn't aware of quite how convenient and comfortable our lives are. The things that bother me can be so petty; the challenges elsewhere feel much more extreme on a daily basis. My gratitude meter has shot way up. And gratitude goes a long way in cultivating all kinds of other goodness.

5. Being forced to do theater again brought up so much. It made me remember why I started doing it in the first place. I remembered the value of collaboration and creative problem solving.

   The experience with the Burkinabe director was incredibly challenging. I really had to put aside my own ego and allow the experience to unfold. Even though he was bossing around the actors and alienating everyone else in the room, I took it as my personal challenge to stay present, alert, and open.

The basic rule in comic improv is "Yes, and…" If you are in a scene and you negate what your partner offers, the scene falls flat and dies. The truth of the scenario is destroyed.

I use this practice in my life, radical "yes-saying" until the scene changes. Eventually it does. When villains fail to destroy, they self-destruct.

So I let the Burkinabe create an oppressive energy in the room without feeling disempowered. It was my choice to let him wreak havoc and see what emerged out of the rubble.

Two days before the performance, he declared he would be leaving early. He would not attend the performance and I was left to improvise a new rehearsal since I had no plan for that day due to his control. Despite that new challenge, I daresay we were all relieved. I was able to work with the actors in an innovative way. Together, we created a piece both unconventional and mesmerizing.

I moved away from theater to pursue other things–namely, my spiritual path. But when I was called on to share theater for a purpose, it was up to me to find the inner resources to step up and accept the challenge. There is definitely meaning in that. If I am here to help the world, then I need to do what is asked of me with whatever I am given. It is that simple.

Journeying On
Some questions for you to investigate:

1. What are your current obstacles?
2. Have you encountered these before?
3. What is the greater meaning you can find in this challenge?

We are on the path of purpose. Look at your challenges and see how they are actually lampposts guiding the way. We have the incredible power to transform our obstacles into opportunities, our personal tragedies into triumphs.

I know this is a place where a lot of stuff will start coming up. All the shadows in our inmost cave need to be aired out before we can transcend. It may feel daunting to undo everything you've been taught to believe about reality. Stick with me. In the next few chapters, we'll go through each myth with a fine-toothed comb and get rid of any thoughts that are mucking up the works. Remember: obstacles are opportunities for growth. When we learn something new, hundreds of thousands of neurons change. This affects our physical body and our physical world. It might hurt, but you will heal. Remember your intentions for being here, and allow them to carry you into the next chapter.

My virtual pilgrim Lisa wrote: "The phrase 'habituated apathy' made me sit up like a prairie dog…. I've often commented over the past two years that I feel 'blah,' like the fire in my belly has gone out and I don't know how to relight it. I realize now that my apathy is simply a habit! Instead of waiting for the fire to be relit, I must *do* things which will ignite my passions again…. To *live with purpose* is something I can do right here, right now…. I had it all backwards…! This all has reminded me that the *doing* is the only thing we have, and it gives us everything."

We will find our way to the center of the labyrinth, and we will be freed.

Chapter 7
THERE IS NO TIME FOR NO TIME

"It's not dying that you need to be afraid of, it's never having lived in the first place."

—The Green Hornet

Ordeal

Before we can emerge victorious from our Journey, we must undergo the necessary changes to destroy what has been holding us back. We must break down The Myths of Time, Money, and Energy. These myths correspond with the next stage in the Hero's Journey: Ordeal, Death, Rebirth. For the purposes of clarity, we will cover one myth with each portion of the Hero's Journey over the next three chapters. This chapter addresses the Ordeal of "Not Enough Time."

Superfriends

Doctor Stephen Strange is a brain surgeon. A brilliant medical doctor. Scientific, logical, and very egotistical. He prides himself on being at the top of his field, which consists of healing people through the conventional means of Western medicine. Yet a near-fatal car accident leaves him with hands that shake uncontrollably, unable to perform surgery, taking away the one thing that has made him who he is. He built his entire identity around something so fleeting. So, too, do we choose stories which limit our ability to connect with the infinite. Our work is tied to our identity–if we had to change it, who would we be? It's precisely through this process that we can find out who we are *meant* to be.

Out of desperation, Doctor Strange goes to Nepal to seek an alternative form of healing from a hermit master known to cure any ailment. This Ancient One teaches him to channel powers far greater than those of the material world. She teaches him to transcend time and space to defeat a great darkness threatening to overtake the world. (These stories do have some common themes.)

When Doctor Strange learns how to create a loophole in time, he is able to trick the whole system. This may seem far-fetched, but quantum physics is proving at this very moment just how malleable time and space are. You, too, have the power to train in ancient arts that will allow you to work with time in new ways. Just as Doctor Strange found a new purpose on the path to self-healing, you too can access powers you never knew you had. You can discover new work that can save the world.

My Ordeal

The first time I had a direct experience with piercing through the Myth of Time was on my very first pilgrimage to Shikoku, Japan. As I mentioned in the beginning of this book, I was completely unprepared in conventional terms. The pilgrimage generally takes 40-60 days on foot. I had not been hiking since I studied abroad in college. I didn't have any clue where I was going or what to expect. My only research consisted of reading two blogs of past pilgrims (one of whom completed it via bicycle). My other resource was a book of maps my friend Jyana gave me. I had a backpack with some clothes and colored pencils which I eventually gave to a pilgrim family with a small child.

You feel every ounce on your back when walking for days. Only take what you need. Consider this a metaphor for life.

I got on the bus to embark on the Shikoku Pilgrimage right before bedtime. When I woke up, I was on an island I hadn't heard of before a week prior.

In theory, this pilgrimage should have been a total failure.

I was at rock bottom in a foreign land. All I knew was that I needed to do things differently than I had ever done them before. So I entered into the pilgrimage with clear intentions:

1. I have pushed myself all my life. I survived and thrived on the frenetic energy of NYC. My vast ambition has caused me to burn out multiple times. I quit that now.

I will go as far as I can go in the 24 days I have. Then, in my remaining three days before Stephanie arrives at my apartment in Tokyo, I will go to the art island of Naoshima. I will listen more and control less. I will go slow. I will practice excruciatingly slow Butoh walking on my way through Shikoku.

I will only go as far as I get. No pushing.

2. I want to spend most of this pilgrimage in quiet, slow solitude. However, if I happen to meet up with other pilgrims, I will follow the custom of traveling with them until it no longer feels right. While I am in their company, I will not push my agenda or pace. Instead, I

will try to understand theirs. If they are walking slower than I want to walk, I will slow down. If they are going faster, I will push myself to keep up unless it is causing me pain or harm. My understanding of the pace of life is not working for me. (Reference: frequent migraines, back pain, and burn-outs.) My intention is to understand time by giving myself over to others. Then, I will reclaim my own pace when the time is right.

3. I will follow my intuition and listen carefully to others. And this, my superfriends, is how we wormhole.

I ended up completing the 1200km pilgrimage in *exactly* 24 days. "How?" you ask. Wormhole. Tesseract. Time bending. Because time and space are not fixed as they seem.

I was first introduced to the notion in the children's novel *A Wrinkle in Time*. Tesseracts are loopholes in time that allow us to travel further distances in faster time. Getting from Point A to C, you usually have to cross Point B–unless you bend time at Point B and A + C fold up to be right next to each other. Then it's just a hop-skip to where you want to be. I now know that tesseracts are very real. We just have to learn how to find them.

What I've learned since that accidental pilgrimage is that it is possible to consciously bend time and space. And to do so is to be the master of one's own universe.

So how do we do this?

Well, my friends, as with all things, it starts with our minds. We have to reprogram how we've been thinking about time because our relationship with it has gotten a little tense. Some of us have become slaves to it like the Mindless Ones of the Marvel Comics universe. Others, like the darklord Dormammu, want to control it completely (and fail). Others think time is running away from us and we are trying to catch it like a White Rabbit down a dark hole. And largely, we are distracted and so we are not nurturing our relationship with it, driving us as crazy as a Mad Hatter. We are not freely swirling in the dance of time of which we are a part.

I did not complete the Shikoku Pilgrimage in 24 days because I am a superhuman. (Well, not physically at least.) It happened because I knew the outcome and set clear intentions.

The power of intention can reorganize your energy in an instant and align you with forces greater than conventional time and space.

Intention + Destination = Wormhole.

Know where you want to go, set your intentions on how you will arrive there, then let the magic happen.

Intentions are one way that the Universe hears your call and brings in your allies to help your noble cause. In Shikoku, for example, I made unexpected friends with a kind Japanese man who owned a *minshuku* (a kind of hotel for pilgrims). I call Hashimoto-san a man, but in reality as I know it, he was an angel. He would randomly drive me around Shikoku in his silver Mercedes Benz and take me to temples from time to time, which allowed me to get farther, faster. We joked because he referred to himself as the Pilgrim Taxi. The Japanese word for taxi is *takushi* and the word for angel is *tenshi*. So I called him the *Tenshi Takushi*–he was my angel taxi.

Hashimoto-san was driven solely by his own motivation to help me finish. Here I was, a stinky, dirty, poor pilgrim riding around in a fancy Mercedes Benz! He would let me out at each temple and tell me in Japanese (for he only spoke Japanese) to "go and do my pilgrim thing." He fed me from time to time and helped me find exceptional places to stay. He never asked me for anything in return. When he'd gone as far as he could go, he would say "Bye bye, I have to go back to work." Later after many days of endless walking, I would get a phone call.

"What are you doing?"

"Still Walking."

"Okay, I'll come get you. Wait at the nearest train station."

And on we would go. There were other companions who helped me along the way, like Ozeki-san who was doing the pilgrimage in honor of his wife who had passed. He was an auto *ohenro*, a pilgrim traveling by car. Ozeki-san talked incessantly for the three days we traveled together, so that it was like being in a perpetual Japanese shower. It broke me. Afterwards, I could miraculously speak Japanese better. Then there was Yamamoto-san who was a walking pilgrim. He convinced me to take the bus and train with him during torrential downpours. I wanted to walk but accepted the invitation. I went with the pace of my comrades no matter what my ego would tell me. And because there was a defined goal and good intentions in place, it worked out more magically than I could have predicted or controlled it if I had tried.

Destroying the Myth of "Not Enough Time"

When I was running the beta course of my Virtual Pilgrimage, I didn't know how I was going to do what I proposed. *Sure, I'll go on a pilgrimage and take people with me virtually!* Then, by the miracle of acting in alignment, people actually wanted to come. *Oh no, well, now what am I going to do?*

When we go off the rails with "crazy" ideas like doing new work after a decade of doing something else, healing ourselves naturally, or transcending time and space, it's easy to fall into the trap of self-doubt. *Who am I to do this?*

But really, who are you not to? If you have the idea, then you already have everything within you to realize it. So we put one step in front of the other and figure it out as we go.

Each time we up-level, that same fear can creep in. So when I was already in the midst of leading the Virtual Pilgrimage, I realized I was attempting to do something impossible. (Again.) I had created a timeline for the course that I couldn't keep up with. There were countless obstacles and reasons why: illness, not accounting for travel days and being offline, not accounting for being in places like India and Africa where being "online" meant something dubious at best. (No uploading videos, I guess. Reroute plans!)

Thus, the days of the Virtual Pilgrimage did not exactly match with the intended schedule. I had to find a way to finish a pilgrimage on time again, while defying conventional notions of time.

"The Law of Intention and The Law of Power are closely related, as they both are the means through which the invisible becomes visible and the unmanifest becomes manifest. Without intention, there is no power. And power, that is not meaningfully channeled through intention, is destructive and can lead to anarchy."
—**Deepak Chopra**, *The Seven Spiritual Laws of Superheroes*

When I worked on my issues with time in a place that seemed timeless like Africa, everything shifted. I realized time is something that we humans totally made up—at least, the way we think about time today. It is a construct.

And if we could create something that has so much power in our lives, that organizes the way our entire world works, we have the power to change it or to create something new.

West African time is a paradox because most things still harken back to the past. Yet the present moment is intensified. I felt like I was transported back in a time machine. For example, you can't get everything you want there. Everything is more simple. There is less pretense, less complication. Because life is about daily survival and dealing with the elements, things are more straightforward.

So things are either happening there, or they are not. When it's hot, people are sleeping. It seems like a universal memo goes out and everyone zonks out. Or if the energy is there, everyone is ready to go. When things are ready, you have to be ready to act or you are left behind. When you have an agenda but it's not the right time, you are going straight to Frustration City if you try to push it through. When it rains, people won't show up for the meeting. When there's a death or sickness, forward momentum stops.

It really challenges my Western world conditioned way of working hard to succeed. If there is a will, there is a way. Rhythms in West Africa correspond more to the earth and paying attention to your body lest you literally burn out into ash.

So how does productivity work in a place like this?

Truth is, it's all about how you feel. Priorities there are super important. You might die this afternoon. If the weather changes, your day's plans might be screwed over. There might be a funeral and everyone will be gone. It might be time for action, and you must be ready.

So you have to decide what is most important to you. There's no space for meaningless activity if you actually want to accomplish something in Diébougou. I had to make so many daily decisions about my priorities. I chose those priorities based on how I wanted to feel.

In Burkina Faso, people live in connection with their feelings and the environment because they have no choice. Every day is a negotiation to survive. In other parts of the world, there seem to be more distractions. There are more trivial tasks and things to grasp for that put us out of alignment. We forget the present moment. We are so conditioned to believe that success lies somewhere outside of ourselves that we forget who we are and what we truly want. When we remember to align with our priorities and engage in practices that bring us into the present, we actually slow down time. We can do more in less time. We do what is really important.

And you know? I finished the Virtual Pilgrimage right on time as well. It wasn't as I had planned, but when I interviewed my pilgrims afterwards, the timing was exactly what each person needed.

Your Hero's Journey: Big Change

Superheroes know that the best actions arise from consciously made choices. What if we made all our choices depending on how we want to feel? We only desire something because of the way we think it will make us feel. So why would we deny our feelings in any realm of our life? Why would we spend so much time at a job that makes us feel anything other than wonderful?

Let's go deeper into our feelings.

1. What are your Core Desired Feelings?

If you haven't decided, decide now. If you've decided already, remind yourself. Close your eyes and feel what it feels like to feel that way. What are the colors, shapes, smells, textures, sounds, images, and sensations in your body when you close your eyes and imagine feeling exactly the ways you want? Really feel what it feels like–it can't just be intellectual; it must be embodied. Call upon this meditation numerous times a day to remind yourself. It only takes minutes and saves you lifetimes of not doing what is aligned with your core.

2. What activities can you do that will make you feel the way you want to feel?

List 5-10 accomplishments or experiences that will make you feel that way. List three things you can do today to generate those feelings. Now do one of those activities immediately. Do not let your subconscious mind talk you out of it with some silly excuse like "I don't have time." or

"I'll do it later." Procrastination does not get us closer to our dreams. It's a surefire way to waste your precious time on this earth.

3. What do you really want?

Make a list. Maybe you want to become a writer or earn 6-figures or own a horse or....

Write down the things you really want to accomplish or own or do. Focus on what you would most love to do for work. Dream specifically about what that looks like. Do *not* censor yourself. Anything is possible here. A trick to manifesting is simply believing that it has already happened. You can trick your brain into creating new pathways as if it already has. Once these pathways are forged, it's only a matter of time before you can achieve it, own it, and be the change. So repeat what you want over and over again until it's yours. Post pictures or post-its around the house. Tell your friends or make a painting of it. Affirm it until there is no question.

And yes! This definitely applies to having work at +10 on the Job Love Meter.

Get super clear and own your desires. Writing them down puts it into contract with the universe. Then, it has no choice but to deliver.

We Can Be Heroes

Doctor Strange wanted desperately to heal. He spent his last penny and put every ounce of his energy into making it happen. This is how he became the "mightiest magician in the cosmos," transcending the multiverse and showing up all over the Marvel Universe.

Living in alignment is what will slow down time so you can be fully present for this life. It comes down to your intentions, desires, and a clear destination. The Universe has its own time signature. If you can release into the infinity of the present moment, anything is possible.

Chapter 8
THE MYTH OF MONEY

"You are much stronger than you think you are. Trust me."
—Superman

Death

Get ready to slay one of the greatest illusions of our modern world. You may feel conquering this illusion is too difficult because we have been programmed through generations to equate money with power. But your real power comes from within.

Superfriends

Think about one of the classic supervillains, Lex Luthor. He is the archenemy of Superman, owner of the corporation LexCorp and driven by wealth, ambition, and power. He is intent on ridding the world of the alien Superman, jealous of his innate power. Lex Luthor is a symbol of the industrial era, of the ability of greed to spin out and dominate all that stands in the way of the ego's control.

Here's the thing: money is not inherently evil.

Money, like all material things on this planet, is made of energy. Quantum physicists are now saying that 99.999999% of the world is made of energy. I'll bet that in a few years, they'll find that it's an even larger percent. I think it's everything. But we humans tend to fixate on the .00001% of the material world instead of the large majority we can't see. We sure spend a lot of time fixating on the acquisition of money–another made-up construct to symbolize the exchange of energy.

Money is no more solid than this computer I am typing on, our bodies, that tree outside, or the dream you had last night. The twenty-dollar bill you hand over to the cashier is made of particles. When you break those down, they are 99.999999% not really there. And yet society puts such an enormous emphasis on money. Thus, we too spend many of our waking (and non-waking) hours consumed by how we can get enough to survive or thrive. The same goes for the material goods we purchase with said currency. Most of us are constantly trying to either get more or spend more so we can have things that aren't even really there (though they sure do appear to be there because of our amazing perceptive and imaginative abilities!)

Here's the miracle shift in thinking: When you start to think of money as another manifestation of your thoughts and energy, you release its greedy grip on your soul.

If you really believed this, would you still keep going to that job you hate every day?

What is the reason you would do anything so soul-damning? Is there any other answer other than: "I need money." For what other reason would we subject ourselves to the pain of not living with purpose? Why wouldn't we retreat into nature or lie on the couch instead of being somewhere we don't want to be? Money. It's a biggie. Are you psyched to destroy this monster illusion once and for all? Money is no more important to understand than Time or Energy, but it can be one of the most liberating to see through. Time and Energy are more ethereal. Less tangible. Time is simply a construct humans have created to stay organized. Energy is the underlying force that makes up all things. But Money? We make it. We deal with it every day. It often guides our decisions. Well, get ready to get liberated. Money is about to become one of your biggest allies.

"Concerning matter, we have been all wrong. What we have called matter is energy, whose vibration has been so lowered as to be perceptible to the senses. There is no matter."
—Albert Einstein

The physical manifestation of Money is a useful tool. We created it as a symbol for an exchange of our energy—the beautiful essence of all that we are. In a conventional scenario, if John works ten hours at an agreed-upon wage, he puts his energy into that timeframe. In exchange, he receives currency as a symbol for the energy he gave to the employer. It is a nice system, but over the years, it became corrupted.

I'm not a historian, but at some point, some humans started thinking that if they had more of this energy than others, they could control them and their environment. They perceived that there was only a certain amount of energy available and they wanted more of a share of the pie. They had not yet heard of quantum physics or understood that the universe is inherently unlimited, so they turned their minds to lack: there is only so much to go around and not enough for everyone.

Those who had more currency yielded this newfound power over those who had less and they, too, began to believe that there wasn't enough for everyone.

But it was a big lie. And you, dear Hero, by reading these words and putting this understanding into practice, will save those oppressed by the system, including yourself! Your newfound power will help others by rippling the knowledge out into the collective consciousness.

Because here is the truth: Energy is unlimited. Money is Energy. Therefore, Money is unlimited. And it is precisely by leaving behind the job that you don't like, that you will discover exactly how that is true for you. You will discover that abundance is creative and not competitive. You will put your unique creative skills to use to uncover the hidden treasure that is available to all who seek it.

Feeling My Own Death

Like most things, I stumbled upon this accidentally while on the Shikoku Pilgrimage. I was about 2/3 of the way to Temple #88 and I had run out of money. I couldn't access an American bank through the ATMs and my Japanese bank account had run out of funds. ATMs on Shikoku are also few and far between. I only had 300¥ and in order to receive the special stamp that you get at every temple, you must pay 200¥. Plus, one makes offerings at every temple. I had one more temple left to visit that day, and no plan as to how I was going to get more money to make all this happen. Plus, I was starving. And tired. And really thirsty.

I happened upon a Japanese *supaa* market. Inside was a marvelous array of prepared foods—sushi, inari, seaweed salad, and ice-cold Ito En green tea. I was standing in front of the display, drooling. In my mind, I tried to work out what I could possibly do to both eat something and make my offering to the temple. *I could buy that inari for 100¥ and then get my stamp for 200¥ and then I could make an extra donation at a later temple… but then what will I do about money for the rest of this*

pilgrimage??? And I guess tea is out of the question? It's sooooo hot. I'm sooooo hungry. Maybe I should just buy the food and quit right here. But then I have no money to get back to Tokyo. I just won't eat. I'll be fine....
And so forth.

As I was standing there, losing my mind and precious minutes of walking daylight, a small elderly Japanese woman walked up to me. I was kind of embarrassed that she caught me in such a compromised position (even if it was only in my mind). But there was such kindness in her eyes that I looked at her and bowed. "*Konnichiwa*," I greeted her. She returned the greeting and in the same moment, pressed a 1000¥ bill into my hands and said, "It's nothing." She bid me to take care on my journey.

I was stunned. I believe I managed to utter a shocked "*arigatougozaimasu*" before she disappeared among the *supaa* aisles. I had enough money to buy food AND green tea AND make a full donation to the temple! I took my inari and a sushi roll and headed to check out.

Of course, she was right there in line. I was able to thank her profusely. Did she know she had saved me? I'm not sure, but it is custom that inhabitants on Shikoku bestow *ossettai* to the pilgrims—a gift to help them along their journey. They believe that by helping pilgrims complete their mission, they also receive the benefits of pilgrimage. I had read about this, but was slightly confused as to why I hadn't experienced it much before that moment. No one had given me oranges or chocolate or money. Then it dawned on me—Hashimoto-san, the other pilgrims, the lady in the supermarket, the people who helped me when I was lost—this was all *ossettai*. I was getting everything I needed, exactly when I needed it.

This did not happen to me because I am any more extraordinary than anyone else. We are all unique and sparkly wonders of the world, but that means that not one of us is more special than anyone else.

Everyone has the same capacity to receive miracles. Every human on this earth has the creative capacity to generate abundance. Every one of us has a unique purpose to fulfill–or else we would not be here.

You too were born with a unique purpose. Everything (including obstacles and the chaos of the world) is here to help guide you to grow into your own power and manifest into a mighty being. You are being tested right now. You are also engaged in a process of deep healing. On the other side is your strength. I promise you this. I look forward to witnessing you emerging as warriors for good.

Your Hero's Journey: Feelings of Death

In Buddhism, there are the concepts of Accumulation and Purification. We accumulate wisdom and merit and purify defilements on the path to enlightenment.

Whether we are Buddhist or not, we perform these two actions all the time. We like to throw out our trash and love collecting goodies. Some of us lean toward one over the other: the collectors and the cleaners. Sometimes in our lives, we stress purifying over accumulating. The physical matter and the actions are manifestations of our energy. Therefore, when we balance the inflow and outflow, we are in clear alignment.

Do you prefer to accumulate or purify?

The truth is that we are always performing these actions simultaneously. When you clean your house, you also receive the benefit of beautifying your environment. These processes are like two wings of a bird–both are absolutely necessary to fly.

> *"As beginners, no matter what we do, our spiritual path will always, crudely speaking, be a path of make-believe.... The advice we are given by the great masters of the past is to start by making the aspiration that one day we will feel genuine renunciation, devotion,*

compassion, etc. By doing so, we accumulate a tremendous amount of merit."

—**Dzongsar Khyentse Rinpoche**,
What to do at India's Buddhist Holy Sites

Our lives are a performance. Working in the theater for so many years, I came to understand what Shakespeare meant when he wrote, "All the world's a stage." We create these dramas in our lives. The things we see around us are the props and the set. The other people are characters we cast in our story. We develop the plot as we continue rehearsing the themes and the dialogue we generate in our minds.

Therefore, if you have Money stories that are causing this play to be a tragedy, it is a great consolation that you are the playwright of your own life. You can change the way this story ends.

Here is an exercise that will make you a Man (or Woman) of Steel:

1. What is your earliest childhood memory of money?
2. What is your current money story?
3. What is the new money story you want to start living?

Most of our beliefs are formed before we are 7 years old. By shining a light on the false fear stories that have no bearing on reality, you can start to rehearse a new act. The more you repeat this new story to yourself, the more this tragedy can transform into triumph.

As a bonus, here is a beautiful and effective practice for transforming your fears around money into love for abundance: Offering Practice. In the Virtual Pilgrimage Course, we did this as a 40-day practice while specifically working through each hero's individual blocks to prosperity. My Virtual Pilgrims were performing this ritual in their own homes as I made offerings with my fellow pilgrims in Bodhgaya. The group accountability and sharing helped process the practice. I was amazed and touched by how deeply this practice worked on the psyches of my Virtual Pilgrims.

To do this practice in your home, first set up a "shrine" area. This is simply a specific area of your space dedicated to the practice. You can make it as elaborate or as simple as you wish, though it helps to decorate it with flowers or any other ornamental items that have spiritual meaning for you. The main thing that you need is a container of some sort. You could use a nice box if you have one. If not, a tissue box or any other box would do, and you could cover it with fabric or foil or magazine cutouts to uplift it. Choose this depository and put it somewhere in your home that you can visit every day.

You will also need "prayer slips." I designed special ones for my Virtual Pilgrims with symbols to facilitate awareness. Get creative! You can design your own or simply cut out slips from plain paper. This is your ritual. Do what inspires you.

What you are to do is write your name, the date, and an aspiration (or wish) on the back of each prayer slip right before visiting your shrine. Include a small monetary donation each time you deposit a slip. Do this for 40 days, once in the morning and once at night.

You can make the offering for a specific person (deceased or living), to an enlightened being or god, or for the general wish that this intention and action contribute to happiness for all beings.

Here is your other objective: make sure to walk a different path each time you visit your shrine, so that you never go the same way twice. One time you may walk around the block to get there, another time you may walk in a direct line from where you start. Play with it. Notice what you are thinking about as you do this.

It is great to do this directly after meditating in the morning or evening, but find your own way! Give meaning to the action.

Offering Practice became one of the most favorite parts for my Virtual Pilgrims. It takes a willingness to show up every day to look at where we are holding on when unnecessary and what we aspire to receive. I am constantly amazed at how profoundly changed I am by this practice. We dedicate many kinds of offerings in the tradition with which I study. When I first started doing offering practice, I asked my friend Sarah why we perform certain mysterious actions. She told me that's how it's done; it's important and we don't have to know why. I found that answer somewhat dissatisfying. However, reflecting on my sustained and developing practice, I love the practice now. It makes so much sense. It has completely transformed my relationship with money and energy. The "why" reveals itself through the doing of it.

There are many different ways we can make offerings and different ways we can tap into spirit in our daily lives. We can give money to beggars on the street, volunteer to feed a bunch of people, or offer food and flowers for enlightenment; likewise, we can meditate, practice self-reflection, study spiritual teachings, or dedicate our lives to serving a cause. The ways we can generate mindfulness, compassion, and faith are infinite. This method consists of using our imaginations to create an environment and practice that allows us to contemplate these qualities.

Destroying the Myth of "Not Enough Money"

I spent Christmas in Burkina Faso while on the Virtual Pilgrimage. Everyone celebrates by putting up some small decoration like one string of lights or maybe a ratty tinsel garland around the doorway. I didn't see anyone give presents except for Miyu (who is not African). Everyone goes around and visits everyone else's home and they eat. It was the first time I had salad in months. It is special for the holiday. I think I ate full meals at five different houses. The day had a feeling of fullness that comes from the celebration of giving and receiving.

However, Christmas seemed to have nothing to do with the consumerism aspects of the event. It may just be the culture, but I imagine it is also because of money. Most people are struggling to buy food on a daily basis. Presents seem excessive in an environment like this.

Africa resembles India in the sense that there is so much perceived poverty around. Kids ask Westerners for handouts nearly constantly. It was a challenging paradox to:

1. Want to give knowing that I come from a more privileged place.
2. Not feel entirely comfortable giving when my own financial stability was questionable.
3. Know that the real issue can't be solved by feeding the world with only the material–that real nourishment comes from within.

So I practiced giving beyond what felt comfortable. I bought candies and gave them to the children who follow me around. I shared my food or drinks with whoever was around. Burkinabe say *"vous êtes invité"* to anyone nearby when they are eating to indicate that they are invited to eat with them. People share what they have there.

I was so ecstatically happy when my host sister Nadi said, "I like your phone… I want your phone." I mean, I couldn't just give her my phone. (I'm not quite there yet.) But I could give her the old phone that I had brought with me in hopes that I could give it to someone in need. Now she has a smartphone that she can connect to wifi at school. She is studying to be a doctor. Now she can do research on her smartphone! What a glorious moment that was.

In Africa and India, I gave and gave past the point I felt comfortable as part of my continued offering practice, to purify my defilements and false thinking around money. Because the only reason I wouldn't give would be because I felt like I didn't have enough.

Believe me when I tell you that I lived this way most my life. My mother grew up super poor in Korea–like carry-your-brother-on-your-back-while-you-walk-five-miles-for-water-without-shoes poor. My father grew up in a family that worked various unglamorous jobs to hold it together (from restaurants to plucking chickens to plumbing, etc.). I grew up hearing the mantra "Money doesn't grow on trees." We were constantly cutting coupons and "saving for a rainy day." My sister Alicia and I were the first in our family to ever graduate from college due to the hard work and dedication of our parents. And while I was blessed with this opportunity, I still inherited a deep poverty mentality, which was not done a great service by choosing to be an artist. It is another culture that has poverty ingrained into its mindset with the "starving artist" paradigm.

I lived thinking that at any moment, I might not have enough to survive or do the work that I knew I was born to do. This caused me to almost kill myself numerous times, burning the candle at both ends (and running the flame all along it to melt it even faster). I was also convinced I needed to "make it on my own," so I was really bad at accepting help from others. I definitely couldn't receive the natural abundance of the universe with a mindset like that.

I thank the gods for the manifestation mindset work and Vajrayana Buddhism that I have been practicing. There are real historical reasons that the majority of humans have come to live in poverty mentality. There are many great books on this, some of which are listed at the end of this one. What we now know is that everything is made of energy; even our thoughts are energy. We use these thoughts to manifest the reality we see. Creative abundance is the primordial state of being and it is our birthright to be fully living in abundance. Nature is totally abundant when we humans quit interfering. However, the majority of humans cannot see that this is the truth. This is why we compete over resources that seem limited. The world currently reflects this destructive way of thinking.

If I say to you, "You can make a million dollars and have the partner of your dreams and travel the world and..._____" (insert what you truly desire here.) If there is any doubt in your mind, or if you get that twinge of "yeah okay, but how?" and especially if you think that something, anything, would be impossible, then you too are living in lack.

It takes a great deal of reprogramming to find the many places in our psyche where we still submit to lack mentality. We have to find these places in ourselves and then root them out like the weeds in our garden. We need to replant them with seeds of what we do want. The more we do this, the more we see our garden flourish and grow. It gets easier and easier to manifest what we want, the more we take the care to do this.

What you desire has already been created. It is waiting for you to call it into being. So after you get really clear on what you want, decide that it is already yours. This is critical. Our psyche has been programmed by various ancestors, lifetimes, and a whole collective unconscious that we have to work with. However, if you decide what you want and that you *will* have it, that in fact, you already do have it, but just don't see it yet, the universe will conspire to work on your behalf. Sending any kind of mixed messages will manifest a mixed bag. Get super clear on what you desire. If your thoughts are a jumble, you will manifest a mess. Meditation comes back in here. Clarifying Core Desired Feelings. Doing Morning Pages to braindump the inevitable buildup in our minds onto the page. Go spend some time alone in nature or walking or gardening or whatever works for you. Do what you can to clear your mind and then get super clear on what you want. Put it on the page in a contract with the universe. Tell the universe that you will have it, no matter what. It wants for us all to be happy.

Superman is not really in Lex Luthor's way. Luthor is in his own way because he perceives things as limited. Decide what you want, sustain that consistent thought over what you actually perceive and be ready to receive. I've been practicing this and it truly works. If it didn't, there would be no possible way that I would be able to spend most of my days traveling the world, practicing spirituality, and making art. Everything–including your dream job–starts in the mind and manifests as miracles. Your thoughts have the power to bring you what makes you feel happy and free and as unlimited as you truly are. So tap into them.

If more people in the world changed their minds from lack to abundance, even in places like Africa and India–where it seems like people couldn't possibly ever have enough–then our lives will begin to change. And so will our work.

When I gave Nadi my phone, I said, "When you decide what you want, and you really ask for it, sometimes it just comes to you. Easy like that." She nodded in agreement.

If it can work for Nadi in Africa, it can work for you too. So decide what you want and then see the creative ways in which it manifests. *Tout est possible!* Anything is possible. Decide for it to be so.

"Chaos everywhere... outside of me. Inside of me, I'm finding more and more calm and focus. A whole bunch of chaos from my past hit me upside the head last Friday and threatened to ruin not only my Christmas with my family, but hobble me financially for most of 2017. Every time I felt panic rising in my solar plexus, something else in my energy system–something newer, something stronger– instantly rose up, defiant, and said, 'You've got this. I've got this. You can do this.' And... I did it! Whatever 'it' was at the moment, I did it. My new mantra is, 'You've got this.'"
—**Lisa Gay Gardner**, Virtual Pilgrim

If you do the 40-day Offering Practice, please let me know by emailing me at sophia@lobsterbird.com. If you share your experience, I will let you know what to do with the money you accumulated from the practice!

Chapter 9

ENERGY IS EVERYTHING

"Our ancestors called it magic, but you call it science. I come from a land where they are one and the same."
—Thor

Rebirth

We have previously discussed how the entire universe is made of energy. This is the truth serum that will reveal the greatest answers to all life's mysteries. In this chapter, we will look at how to apply this knowledge to your life so that you can transcend any pain and suffering you may feel.

Superfriends

It's like Charles Xavier from The X-Men. He may be "crippled" and bound to his wheelchair, but he is one of the most powerful of mutants.

He used the power of his mind to reach beyond his physical limitations to create a school that trains young mutants to harness their superpowers. He fosters a supportive community that serves other like-minded souls who are oppressed by society.

You too can transcend limited notions of the body by using the power of your mind. You will heal, and you will help others heal by so doing.

Your Hero's Journey: Feelings of Life

Bodies, like Money, are a practical area where people get stuck in limited thinking. It has become the norm for people to feel tired, unmotivated, achy, low energy, or even to tolerate huge amounts of pain on a daily basis. Some act as though our bodies are actually enemies on our journey to our greater destiny. I hear people condemning their bodies in casual conversation. Many spiritual traditions misleadingly attempt to transcend the body. While I believe that the latter is totally possible, we don't transcend anything by pretending it's not there or by beating it to death. It is through love that all things are transformed, and that includes our physical Body.

Our bodies are critical in the realm of work. While our minds are responsible for the actions our bodies perform, there are few jobs we could do without our physical bodies. (That is, until the impending Technological Singularity renders our bodies useless, scheduled loosely for the year 2050.) In fact, our minds and energy are really what cause us to get up and go to work every day, and our bodies are the vehicles for creating action. It's quite amazing what some people have done despite the most extreme physical limitations, such as one of my mentors Jon Morrow, who is paralyzed from head-to-toe with the exception of his mouth. He uses this very smart mouth to channel the energy to run a multimillion-dollar company that he built from his wheelchair. He is one of the top bloggers on the internet. That's a lot for someone whose body seems limited.

His story implies that there is no physical excuse for not pursuing greatness. Think about other champions such as Lance Armstrong or Christopher Reeve, who transcended their dis-abilities and dis-ease to be highly able. Without the power of their minds and energy, they would not have been able to help countless others conquer their own obstacles.

Whatever your excuse is, are you ready to get rid of it? Because here's the thing: you can work with whatever is going on for you right now. It is most likely *the exact path* to the great life's work you are meant to create. Illness inspired Armstrong to create Livestrong to help countless people with cancer; Christopher Reeve brought awareness and new technologies to paralysis and neurological disorders; Jon Morrow is now helping young bloggers use their words to help others. Will you leverage your story to help others or let it take you down?

But here's the amazing news: there are ways to heal naturally from many of the things that are causing pain, discomfort, and dis-ease in our bodies. One of the critical elements of my Hero's Way program is the energy healing people receive while creating their business ideas. A lot of our illness is the result of psychic pain.

Therefore, healing and self-care are critical to your entire psyche. If you are going to do something as dramatic as transitioning out of a job you hate, moving to be in a happier space, getting into a life-long partnership with a loved one, or in any other way transforming your life, you must become a master of self-care. It is another superpower and we must put ourselves in training to realize it.

"If you want to find the secrets of the universe, think in terms of energy, frequency and vibration."
—Nikola Tesla

Our body is made of energy. Neuroscientists have this great saying, "Where attention goes, energy flows." When we put conscious attention on caring for our bodies instead of hating them, ignoring them, or unconsciously mistreating them, we will receive an equivalent energy back from our bodies. In a very practical way, if you decrease the amount of toxins increase the amount of healthy nutrients, your body will feel better. If you increase activity that decreases stress and generates wellness, your body will feel better. If you find ways to shield yourself from electromagnetic stress and engage in energy that stimulates homeostatic activity, your body will heal itself and it will feel better. These are very practical side-effects of self-care.

On a deeper level, how you view your energy is enough to set these practical changes in motion without feeling like you are forcing yourself to be healthy. If you focus on how tired you are or how you get headaches that prevent you from working, your brain hardwires itself to think that those conditions are a reality that frequently occurs. The more you think about them, the more frequently your brain sends signals to your body to ensure they continue, and increase in frequency! This is likely the opposite of what any of us would like. Therefore, we have to address both the inner and outer conditions that are causing the discomfort. I read this passage while on pilgrimage in India:

"Bodhgaya is not only special because it's where all the buddhas will achieve enlightenment. According to Tantric Buddhism, everywhere in this world and all the phenomena that exists outside ourselves have a corresponding existence within our bodies. Good practitioners and yogis are able, in their practice, to visit the holy places that reside within the chakras and channels of their own bodies, and in this way make progress on their path to enlightenment. Those of

us whose practice isn't quite so advanced can at least visit the outer reflection of these inner holy sites."

—**Dzongsar Khyentse Rinpoche**,
What to do at India's Buddhist Holy Sites

In this way, I've designed the Hero's Way to visit the holy sites within ourselves and turn our work into our ministry.

Whip out your journal and freewrite for 5 minutes on this prompt: "If I were energy—which I am—I would..."

My Rebirth

When I was in Japan, right before Jyana and Earl told me about the Shikoku Pilgrimage, I was in serious pain. Everything in my life was crashing down around me and my psyche shut my body down right along with it.

Seven years prior, I had suffered a stress injury that would chronically resurface every time I got myself into similarly stressful situations. I was living in the East Village, and creating a dance performance combining Shakespeare's *Twelfth Night* and Beyoncé's high-octane "Single Ladies" dance. I was working overtime at three different karaoke bars to make enough money to pay my rent and eat ramen noodles (not the fancy Japanese kind). I had a film audition on this particular morning that I had to record. But I was exhausted and overslept my alarm.

When I noticed the time, I shot up in bed. Simultaneously, a searing pain shot up from below my left shoulder blade into my neck and brain. I fell back down onto the bed and couldn't move. I was paralyzed.

My roommate had a tendency to leave and visit her family for days, so no one else was in the apartment. I did not know when she would return. My cell phone was inches away from my left hand. But try as I might, I could not move to reach it. It was the first of many times where I thought, "I might just die here, alone and in pain."

I clearly didn't die (at least not in the physical sense), but this situation would recur throughout the next 7 years in various ways.

Fast forward to Japan, and I was in the same situation. I was laid out on the floor, pain surging through my neck and back, unable to move. In the midst of all the chaos of my life falling apart, my collaborator had asked me, "Do you know who Alan Watts is?"

I didn't think much of it at the time, but as I laid there for days on end, I kept hearing his voice repeat the same question: *Do you know who Alan Watts is?*

I thought: *If this is the time I do die alone and in pain, at least I get to trip out before I go.*

And I did. I was able to move enough to find countless Youtube lectures by Sir Watts and I listened to them for weeks between long bouts of breathing and crying.

I didn't know it at the time, but this was a period of self-care. I was opening up to ideas about reality that were beyond any ideas I had ever had. I was not pushing myself to be out dancing and eating in Tokyo. I was resting and recovering. It had taken yet another complete shutdown to force me to do so.

By the end of two weeks, I was well enough to go see Jyana's Bunraku chanting performance. Turns out, Jyana's dad was friends with Alan Watts. He's a professor of Buddhism, and she asked me, "Have you ever heard of the Shikoku Pilgrimage?"

A week later, I was on my way. You can imagine the condition I was in.

About 1/4 of the way through the pilgrimage, my right knee started to throb tremendously. Pilgrim Angel Ozeki-san had driven me in his car for three days, so I had a brief reprieve. But once I was on my own walking again, I couldn't deny that something would have to give. I'd either have to stop or my knee would.

I decided once and for all to listen to and respect the wishes of my body.

My sister, Alicia, had given me a guidebook for travel in Japan. I had only looked at it once, but was intrigued by this place in Shikoku called Ohki Beach. It's a famous spot for surfers. The description of Kaiyu resort sounded so wonderful. It was an environmentally sustainable resort with natural *onsen* baths, a kind and hospitable owner named Mitsu, amidst a nature preserve. It was totally out of my league and price range, considering my finances were one of many things that had come crashing down in flames. It was also off-the-beaten pilgrimage trail, so I would have to go out of my way to get there. Yet I could not ignore my body any longer nor the voice in my head that persisted in telling me, "Just go there. You have to go there."

Thus, I went. I would later find out that voice is called a "spirit guide." Should yours miraculously appear and start guiding you, I highly encourage you to listen. It leads to all kinds of miracles.

My time at Kaiyu was completely magical. What happened at Okhi Beach is a whole other book. In short, I ended up working for Mitsu for three days, being fed organic meals fit for royalty, receiving a visit from my sea turtle spirit animal, and having profound realizations about my life. Plus, the natural springs healed my knee completely. I was better than ever for having attended to myself and my intuition.

And if you think about it, I took three days off from the pilgrimage to stay at Kaiyu. That means I actually completed the pilgrimage part of it in 21 days. Miracles!

One other tremendous healing encounter happened post-pilgrimage:

Alicia came to visit me for a month after the pilgrimage. We traveled to Aomori, in the northern part of Japan, to meet Mari Osanai. Mari is another angel, a dancer who teaches *Noguchi Taiso*. I was sent to learn this gentle and powerful movement practice and I brought Alicia along for the lesson.

While we were there, Alicia's back went out in a major way. She could barely move. So Mari took us to see Dr. Fujiya, an acupuncturist known for being a miracle worker. I received a treatment for my neck and back, and during the session he asked me if he could put his hands on me. If it were any other doctor, I might have been creeped out, but he had such a kind, gentle air about him. (Hint: angels are everywhere.) Plus, Mari was there with me, so I felt extra protected.

Turns out, Dr. Fujiya performed Reiki on me. It was the first I had ever heard of Reiki, which is an energy healing modality that rebalances a person's electromagnetic energy. It is both an ancient healing art and currently being reconfirmed as a legitimate healing modality by scientists who study the human energy field. All I knew at the time was that I felt truly healed.

When I returned to the U.S. several weeks later, I was having a visceral bodily reaction every time I considered returning to NY. My whole body would tense up at the slightest thought of moving back. So I decided to stay with my parents for awhile, while life continued its glorious unraveling. At that time, my Aunt Chongae was sent to the hospital for serious heart surgery. She was stressed out to the max, not sleeping in the hospital, and was too underweight for them to perform the surgery (thus prolonging her hospital stay and perpetuating the problem). It did not look like she would survive the surgery in this state.

When I saw her, I heard that voice again. It said, "Put your hands on her." I was slightly terrified. *What if she freaks out? What if my family thinks I'm a freak?* But someone had to do *something*. The doctors and our family all thought she might die during the surgery if she entered it in her current state. So, I did it. I put my hands on her and hummed. She promptly fell asleep for the first time in days. My parents were stunned. I was stunned. She made it through the surgery and went home soon after.

Then, apropos of seemingly nothing, trusted friends and mentors kept mentioning that I should learn Reiki. Because of my experience with Aunt Chongae in the hospital and Dr. Fujiya in Aomori, I found my teacher and abruptly set on the path to becoming a Reiki Master. The healing power of energy broke me of the illusion that our physical bodies are the be-all, end-all of our human existence. I have since learned many energetic healing modalities that I combine into a unique practice. As I continue to work with clients and witness miracles, I hope to share its power with as many as will receive it. I do deep work channeling the earth's energy fields to understand how we are all connected. I think it's about time we all learned to work together again.

And by the way, I've never had my neck or back go out again since.

Destroying the Myth of "Not Enough Energy"

Working with energy unexpectedly became my life's work. It often does once people realize its tremendous healing power. In my Hero's Way program, I give weekly energy healings to my clients. As they are releasing blocks and realigning their energy, they come into the experience of the unlimited energy of the Universe, and at a live retreat, they can learn energy healing for themselves and those they are meant to serve. The energy multiplies as more people share in moving it!

When we build our plans from a state of balance and inspiration, what we create is so much more resonant. It comes from our deepest source of all that we are–unbounded energy.

Chapter 10

SEIZE YOUR JUST REWARD!

"Life doesn't give us purpose. We give life purpose."
—The Flash

Reward–Seizing the Sword

This is where things start to get really fun. If you've made it this far, then you have slain the dragon guarding the cave. We've gone through the Ordeal, Death, and Rebirth of our Hero's Journey. I told you about the many times I almost died in this lifetime and we looked into our individual shadows to find the fear that has been ruling our lives. We investigated this through the three big Myths of Not Enough Time, Money, and Energy. We found that all of those are excuses that keep us small; they keep us from playing big and receiving in accord.

Remember: it is impossible to not have enough of anything when everything is limitless.

That means you are ready to receive your treasure! This is the point of accepting big change and vast rewards.

So, are you clear on the excuses you've been making about doing the work you are meant for? Are you clear on the false beliefs that have been holding you back?

It's critical to go through the process of looking directly at our fears and recognizing them for the illusions that they are. I know they feel very real when they are happening to us. But the more you shine a light on them, the more you will see that the monsters lurking around your bedroom are simply shadows waiting to be illuminated for what they really are.

I like to hug my monsters, nestling into their thick, furry bodies, risking death by ferocious claws and teeth. All too often, the monsters I feared disintegrate the moment I embrace them. They always remain with me in my memories, but the moment of the hug–how it feels to sink right into them with love–is what remains. That and the joy that comes from knowing they can't scare me ever again.

Superfriends

In *Monsters, Inc.*, the energy source for the city of Monstropolis is fueled by the screams of human children. The monsters that work in the factory are called "scarers" and they sneak into the bedrooms of children at night to harvest their screams. It is considered dangerous work because children are considered "toxic." However, Monstropolis is facing an energy crisis because children are no longer as easily scared as in times past.

When a door is mistakenly left activated on a scare floor, a small girl sneaks into the factory. In the process of trying to return the girl home, Mike and Sulley realize she's not toxic. The young girl's affection towards the monsters disarms them. They're not so bad either. A whole world operating off fear changes when they solve the energy crisis with their friendship. Turns out, children's laughter is a far more powerful energy source than fear.

This is the process of purification in action. The more we let go of our false beliefs, the more merit we are able to accumulate. The more we clear our conditioning that prevents us from loving conditionally, the friendlier the world becomes. The more we are able to clear a space for awareness in our own minds and hearts, the more we can fill it with new ideas, creativity, and a brighter reality.

Your Hero's Journey: Accepting the Consequences of New Life

Now, I know a lot of people who have tried manifesting and it didn't work. Law of Attraction, prayer, and various New Age metaphysical practices did not yield the results that they wanted to see in their material world. I think that's because of human consciousness has recently evolved to a point where we can now understand it from a scientific viewpoint. And it's actually *not* as simple as thinking it into being.

Here are my 5 Steps for Manifesting Greatness:

1. Meditate
2. Purify
3. Dream
4. Reconnect
5. Accumulate

We have gone through the first two steps:

1. Meditate

We need to change our brain states from Beta, where we are in a constant state of fearful reaction to our environment to Alpha waves states and higher. This is where we can have a greater awareness of our conditioning. We can enter into the subconscious, make changes, and have more control over the outcomes. Otherwise, we remain trapped in a mind state that is keeping us prisoner.

2. Purify, Purify, Purify

Investigate all the fear stories, habits, and negative thought patterns that are keeping you stuck exactly where you don't want to be. Declare your change. Practice letting go and offering them to a source of your own choosing.

Here is the next step:

3. Dream (the Impossible Dream)

After that, we begin to dream. It's like painting on a blank canvas instead of one that someone has already painted on and then dumped in a dumpster. Get out your Zen Beginner's Mind again.

Get in touch with what moves you, what lights you up. What makes you feel most alive??

I find that there are generally two groups of people that get to this stage:

1. Those who have tried manifesting and it didn't work.
2. Those who have never given themselves permission to declare what they really want.

In the latter category, maybe no one has ever asked them. Maybe they were blessed to have life's flow be relatively easy, and so they simply went with it. Whatever the reason, there is no judgment. However, we all have a dream in our hearts. A lot of times it is squelched at an early age. Children are criticized by adults who themselves were not allowed to dream. Or the conventional world would say it's impossible for, say, a child growing up in the slums of India to become a wealthy Bollywood movie star. And, yes, conventionally, that would seem rather difficult. However, you and I, my dear superfriend, are beyond thinking about things conventionally at this point.

You have the Universe's permission in this moment, right now: Dream!!! And DREAM BIG!!!

What is it you really want? What makes your heart sing?

Another sticky situation is that we often allow ourselves to dream within the confines of a false reality. We say we want a thousand dollars when, really, we want a million. But to the Universe, there's no difference. They are just zeros. Big or small, the Universe wants you to be happy. The Universe is the closest thing we have to understanding love. It's the cycles of creation and destruction calling forth whatever we ask of it.

What would you ask for if you knew you could have anything? Make a list of everything you want. Do not limit yourself. Be honest with your heart's desires. Dream onto the page.

We Can Be Heroes

Where would we be if Martin Luther King, Jr. never dared to dream? He made it his life's work to create a more equal world. Can you start to dream about the world you want to see?

The Hero's Journey is not something relegated to fiction. You can find this arc throughout your lifetime and you can use it to create a new story. It just depends on how big you dare to dream.

So write it down now. Do it again and again. Dream bigger each and every time.

Finish this sentence: "I have a dream…"

"I have a dream…"

"I have a dream…"

Finish this sentence until there are no more dreams left. Write dreams for yourself. How much money do you want to make? What do you want to do for a living? How do you want to be *living?* Where in the world do you want to go? What changes do you want to see in the world? What do you dream about for this world???

This is how our prayers and wishes develop. Once we allow ourselves to dream for what we want on small levels, then we can dream bigger. Once we allow ourselves to dream of what we truly desire, we can be free to make wishes on behalf of the world.

Our desires are not selfish. They are the seeds for planting a better world, one where we are all abundant, and we are all free.

Have you read Dr. King's speech lately? He wants his kids to go to school like other kids, and he also wants a world of freedom for all people.

> *"I have a dream that my four little children will one day live in a nation where they will not be judged by the color of their skin but by the content of their character.... I have a dream that one day every valley shall be exalted, and every hill and mountain shall be made low, the rough places will be made plain, and the crooked places will be made straight; 'and the glory of the Lord shall be revealed and all flesh shall see it together.'"*
> **—Dr. Martin Luther King, Jr.**

He addresses the lack mentality that kept true equality from balancing out the color contrast in the American nation. We've made large strides since then, but it's still pervasive in our society. And this isn't just an American problem. This exists all over the world. It's no longer a question of national boundaries. The *Universe* is abundant. In this vast space, there should be no one who suffers from false promises and beliefs.

"We refuse to believe that the bank of justice is bankrupt. We refuse to believe that there are insufficient funds in the great vaults of opportunity of this nation. And so, we've come to cash this check, a check that will give us upon demand the riches of freedom and the security of justice. We have also come to this hallowed spot to remind America of the fierce urgency of Now."
—Dr. Martin Luther King, Jr.

All you have is *now*, Heroes. What are you going to do with this one precious moment? Are you going to allow yourself to stay small and stuck? Or are you going to dream bigger for a better world?

It all starts in your mind. Your thoughts shape reality. The more of us who consciously create our own lives, the more quickly the collective consciousness conspires for true transformation and freedom.

The next step to Manifesting Greatness is:

4. Reconnecting.

This means two things:

A. Forging new neural pathways in the brain so we can become the person we want to be.
B. Forging a new connection with the divine.

Your thoughts *are* important. They shape new pathways through repetition of new desires. However, there is a magic trick to manifesting that will allow you to bypass a lot of the conscious neural reprogramming process. The trick is: instead of thinking about what you want, start being the person who has it. If you want to feel a certain way, *act* as if it's already done. Life is a performance, remember? The more you rehearse it, the more real it becomes. If you start acting in alignment with your

Core Desired Feelings, you will ninja-style reprogram your *subconscious* mind. When you can be it, you will see it. This feels like touching in with the divine.

Seizing My Sword

I love all spiritual traditions because at their very source, they all say the same thing: We are God. We are the Universe. All things are made of the same energy, and that energy is love. What we seek is also seeking us. We simply need to hit the mark with the arrow of our intention.

As children, Alicia and I attended the Lutheran Church of the Holy Spirit very intensely by our parents' request. We went to church every Sunday. When we were old enough, we also went to Youth Group on Tuesday evenings. I babysat in the nursery during services. I played my clarinet for the congregation for special holiday services. I acted in the yearly Nativity Play (playing every role from shepherd to angel to king). I discovered a treasure chest full of hand puppets in the attic and then proceeded to convince our youth leaders to let us use them again. We went out in the community to nursing homes and performed for the congregation. Considering my level of involvement in the church, I found many things about Christianity challenging to accept fully.

I remembered all this when I landed at a Christian church service in West Africa while leading the Virtual Pilgrimage. I was laughing because in some weird way I keep being asked to relate my spiritual ideas and tell stories of my journeys. Since I believe that the Sacred World is this one right here, I might as well be reading Bible stories when I relate my own. I am preaching to a new choir of heroes that will create spiritual relationships of their own understanding. Gone is the age of organized religions competing over truth. I find the Christian religion to be generally positive, but it was born out of thousands of years of patriarchy mindset. We are moving into a new time where we can overcome our ego's conditioning to feel separate, and honor our deep connection with all things. As humans, we use stories to help us understand the world. The Bible has helped numerous people understand kindness and find faith in the mysterious. Alicia once reminded my father and me that Jesus himself said he can't be found within the walls of the church but everywhere and in everyone. This is pieced together from various books of the Bible:

> *"The Most High does not dwell in houses made with hands...*
> *Behold, the Kingdom of God is within you.*
> *I am the light that is over all things. I am all: from me all came*
> *forth, and to me all attained. Split a piece of wood; I am there.*
> *Lift up the stone, and you will find me there."*
> **—Jesus Christ**

We are not human beings seeking spirit but rather spirit manifested in human form. Even Jesus said:

> *"If the flesh came into being because of the spirit, it is a wonder.*
> *But if the spirit (came into being) because of the body, it is a*
> *wonder of wonders.*
> *Yet I marvel at how this great wealth has taken up residence in*
> *this poverty."*

In so many ways, Jesus keeps saying that we *are* the light. Our problem is that we are blinded from our own being and that makes us feel poor. It causes us to live in poverty and embody lack. We must look within to discover the Sacred World, which is all that we are.

Like Bible stories have done for so many, our own stories can be the most powerful form of transmission we have to remind ourselves of our true nature. That is why it is incredibly important to purify those negative stories that we have developed over the course of this human life and write the story we are meant to live.

This leads to the final step:

5. Accumulate your riches.

Accumulate new stories, ones that reflect the world that you want to live in.

My relationship with spirituality deepened and clarified during my time in West Africa. They leave so much up to God's will. One thing that became certain is that God is not some old guy on a throne dictating how everything will turn out. He is in everything, including all of us.

In Japan, it is common belief that everything has 気 (*ki*) or spirit. I believe this too. God is energy. All things are made of energy. That means you are God. I am God. All is God. And the only thing stopping us from recognizing our own God-force is the limits of our own minds.

So get out of the way and let God flow through you! The power feels good and it is good for us all.

I think of this as the Bow and Arrow of Flexible Persistence. We can find this new weapon hidden amongst the treasures within our cave. Your desires will lead you to your purpose. They will help you find the work you are meant for. Hold them tight. Focus on the way you want most to feel. Most of us skip this step on the path of life. And no wonder, because the mapmakers have left it out of the cartography for so many years. If we want to blaze new trails, we must clear this channel close to home. Then, we can hit the mark of our final destination.

When you are being who you want to be despite what the world tells you, when you are doing what you love no matter what adversity arises, stay the course with dedication. Know that in order to hit your target, you must bend the strings. You must release at the right moment. Trust the wind to carry your arrow to the center.

It doesn't have to be hard when you find this balance of focus and ease. There are insistent forces we must battle: the monotony of life when not living with passion; searching for one's way in the great dark unknown without an internal compass; living one's life out of alignment. The force of imbalance causes a lot of injury, pain, and distortion. We see it happen in people's bodies as they age; we feel it in our souls every day.

But you, my dear Hero, have your Bow and Arrow of Flexible Persistence. It will aid you along many more trials and adventures to come. The flexibility of the bow will give you the ability to adapt and thrive. The directness of your arrow will give you strength and confidence to persevere. And you may very well be surprised by the agility and ease by which you come to hit the magic mark time and time again.

Happy target practice!

"The Virtual Pilgrimage made me more accountable of how I want to feel and doing what I needed to feel that way. Having you there every step of the way, even though you were physically miles away, was awesome…. It's all about being happy with what you're doing, and on your terms, and being able to sustain the way you want to live. I feel thankful to God every morning for the day."
—Stephanie Juen, Virtual Pilgrim

Chapter 11

YOU ARE IN CHARGE

"The strength of this country isn't in buildings of brick and steel. It's in the hearts of those who have sworn to fight for its freedom."
—Captain America

The Road Back

My dear Hero, we are scheduled to depart soon from the horrors and ecstasies of Special World. If you have accepted the consequences of this new life, you are ready for the Road Back to Ordinary World. Here, you will be able to share your gifts with the world you had temporarily left behind. Ordinary World may seem the same, but you, my friend, have changed. Therefore, it too will change to reorganize around the new you.

But before you can return safely to the Shire, you will face some last-minute dangers that threaten to derail you from fully completing the circle. These obstacles may seem like new challenges, but they are, in fact, your old fear stories coming up with clever new adaptations to trick you into giving up and dying a slow, painful death in Special World.

"It's helpful to keep in mind that the world is your classroom and other people are your assignments. Every experience you perceive on the movie screen that is your life gives rise to one of two choices: to learn through the perception of love or to learn through the perception of fear. Each instance is a holy encounter providing a divine spiritual assignment in which you can choose to heal or stay stuck in the bondage of your past. If you choose to show up for these Universal Assignments with a willingness to heal, then many miracles will be presented to you. But if you're unwilling to show up for these assignments, you will stay stuck in the stories and experiences that do not serve you."

—**Gabrielle Bernstein**, *The Universe Has Your Back*

I started reading Gabby's book before I left on the pilgrimage. I was astounded by the clarity of her process and her unabashed, unwavering commitment to transforming fear into faith. She is a student of *A Course in Miracles*, which details how our greatest obstacles are really Universal Assignments that are designed to guide us to our ultimate healing. When we are living with purpose and guided by the love of the Universe, our divine occupation unfolds naturally before us. Our careers become our ministry to spread our message of light into the world.

The Universe is here to guide you, but only you can make the choice to change your perceptions from fear into love. You have all the power within you to do this, and it is especially important to face your last-minute obstacles with a newfound dedication to overcoming them. This is where many people fail and drop off. I warn you of this danger now so that you can face it head on and slay the demons once and for all.

You can reconnect with your power by recognizing when the fear story arises, and changing that story to love. Meditate to give that story some space. Practice letting go to clear the movie screen. Focus on the story you *want* to see unfold. Project that onto the screen in your mind's eye.

> *"The moment you notice yourself disconnected from the feeling of your power, you can change the reel. Through the power of your intentions, you can reorganize your energy in an instant. Remember that your intentions create your reality."*
> —**Gabrielle Bernstein**, *The Universe Has Your Back*

It is time we reflect on our original intentions for embarking on the journey in the first place. Are you the same person as when you started? Are you facing the same struggles and obstacles? Do they seem different, but are simply disguised in a different hat? Or maybe you are soaring on the energy that you've been cultivating throughout this journey and you feel unstoppable. Wherever you may be, it is possible that you will also encounter: Last-Minute Danger.

Superfriends

Where would Spain be if Don Quixote simply took the world for what it was, instead of imagining a new story? It is a tale both comic and tragic.

Nearing his 50s, Don Quixote decides to become a knight-errant in search of adventure. He decides to live the stories he loves. We love the quixotic hero for his dedication to romance and chivalry. The tragedy of Don Quixote's story is that he gives up right before the end. His cherished adventure books are burnt, and he is convinced by his housekeeper to return to bed instead of retiring in the countryside as he wishes. He returns to "sanity" and renounces his previous ambition. Illness, death, sadness.

What is it all for if we don't fully follow through to the end?

My Road Back

As I was about to merge back into Ordinary World after the Shikoku Pilgrimage, I encountered a serious Last-Minute Danger. I had to fight my old inner demons that wanted to pull me back and prevent me from really bringing it home.

Here's what happened:

It was the final day of my pilgrimage. I had one full day to get to the last temple, #88, which is a long hike up a steep mountain. I estimated that it would take about 6–8 hours walking. I was alone again. Hashimoto-san had dropped me off the day before, strongly urging me to take the bus to the final temple.

I decided to listen, as it is wise to listen to spirit guides when they give you advice. However, when I arrived at the bus station in the wee hours of the morning, the bus didn't come according to the posted schedule. This was extremely odd. Japanese transportation systems are rarely ever a minute off schedule. So I waited. There was no one else around. So, I waited some more. Then I realized, *if I keep waiting, I don't know when the bus will come. I am wasting precious walking time. I need to get to the temple before the last bus leaves to drive down to the city where I need to board my evening train. I have to go now.*

So I headed off on foot.

I walked for many hours through many towns. I was invited in for tea by a sweet lady who showed me a newspaper clipping of an interview she did about the pilgrimage. I met another woman in a supermarket who was super inspired by what I was doing. She told me to write my blog in Japanese so she could read it. I was sailing on happy wings.

I ended up at this amazing place, The Pilgrim Welcome Center. Who knew such a magical place existed? They had a whole art installation replete with interactive diorama. There were free beverages and snacks.

They gave me an official certificate of completion and told me that I might be able to do important work sharing my experience in English and Japanese. And then, they told me I was headed off into the final and hardest part—the mountain. Once you start going up, you must keep going or you'll have to come back down the same way. *I had come this far, what could stop me now?* I embarked with a fearless attitude and open heart.

I walked for many miles up the steep mountain path. Every so often, there was a little bird on the path. I would watch it and as I approached, it would fly out of my way and land a bit further down the path. Land. Walk, walk, walk. Fly a bit. Land. Walk, walk, walk. It continued like this for awhile. Then, I looked down the path for the little bird. But there was something big in the path. *This is not a bird. What is it?* It was hairy and big. As I got closer, I realized it was over half my size. *What the heck is that??*

As I approached about a couple yards away, it turned to face me—it was a giant and unhappy-looking mountain monkey! *What?!? I had read about wild boars and snakes and all kinds of other things, but no one mentioned rabid mountain monkeys!!!* It started screaming at me. Something way deep inside me activated.

In a moment, I realized I had no choice but to continue moving forward. To my left was solid mountain wall. To my right, a tree-lined cliff headed straight down to a death fall. The only other option was to retreat back down the mountain, not finish the pilgrimage, and possibly get chased by it anyway. I kid you not, I had a bag of food hanging off the side of my pack and there was a banana inside. I decided the only way was through.

I felt this charge surge up inside me—this reservoir of energy that had seemed dormant or untapped. It was as if it all condensed into my center and I knew exactly what I had to do. *I have to Butoh-walk slowly towards Monkey Demon holding my walking stick in front of me like a martial arts weapon and send it a message of peaceful yet firm insistence that it get the heck out of my way because I am coming.* There was no stopping me. I started to move straight for it as if parting an ocean of molasses. In Japanese I said, "Monkey-san, I need you to let me pass. I will not hurt you. I am a friend. But I am coming, so let me pass. Please." I didn't dare take my eyes or my energy off Monkey-san. I just kept walking towards him with a confidence I had never felt in my life.

When I would get too close, he would run further down the path until we were the same distance apart we started at. Then he would turn and scream at me some more. I kept on walking. Monkey-san: run, turn, scream. Me: walking steadily. Monkey-san: run, turn, scream. Repeat.

I thought this could go on forever. The other alternative was that Monkey-san's friends were well on their way for a group attack and I was finished. There was still no way but forward.

After many turns, Monkey-san screamed at me and jumped through the trees and off to the right. *Okay, for sure his entire family is going to bust out of there as I walk by and overtake me.* I locked my gaze straight-forward and continued anyway. I figured, *what is the worst that could happen? If I get attacked by a group of angry monkeys and die here in Shikoku on the way to the last temple of the pilgrimage, I can honestly think of no better way to go. So why not do it like a badass?* I resumed molasses walk towards the end goal.

As I passed the trees where Monkey-san had disappeared, I slowly turned to see his big ol' monkey face poking out of the foliage. He could have easily jumped out and taken me out from the side. Instead, he was now making these little chirpy monkey coos and watching me slow-walk my way to destiny.

I said, "*Arigatougozaimasu, Saru-San.*" Thank you, Monkey-san. And thank you to all the other gods who were protecting me along this journey. Just past Monkey-san's exit was a roadside set of Buddha statues. I offered up my lemon soda as a token of my gratitude.

From there, it was smooth sailing to the art island of Naoshima and to finding loads more inner strength and purpose. I have never considered turning back down that mountain again.

I tell you this story to prepare you for what's coming. Some force beyond my knowing was mustered up to battle Monkey-san (peacefully) and now I know precisely what was happening.

It all boils down to this:

We create this world with our minds. As we grow ever closer to merging our deepest dreams with the world we see around us, our subconscious will do everything in its power to try and stop us. It will dredge up our deepest fears. It will create false obstacles where there really are none. You will need to recognize this when you see it and continue boldly forward. Focus on your end goal, and know that the only way is forward.

Your true work awaits. I look forward to your triumphant return home, Hero! Onward and upward!

Your Hero's Journey: New Challenge and Rededication
Opportunity to Scribe:

1. What obstacles are you facing now? Can you see how they are a manifestation of your old obstacles in new forms?
2. What last-minute danger have you encountered that is trying to stop you from really bringing this home?

One way this can show up is in the form of a healing crisis. When we are in a process of natural healing, there is generally a flare up of the existing condition. It gets worse before the healing process stabilizes. Sometimes new conditions arise to freak you out. It is easy to panic and feel like things are getting worse. This only worsens the condition. Accessing your intuition and understanding that it is part of the curative process is key. Keep calm and carry on.

My Journey Continues

When I returned to NYC on The Road Back from the Virtual Pilgrimage, it was January 20th, 2017. I rolled up to Jayme's apartment after a long, hot African bus ride and four flights from Ouagadougou to Ethiopia to Paris to New York. I had been traveling for days but arrived in the morning. Jayme and I hadn't seen each other in months and there was much to catch up on. We talked all day until I passed out on her sofa bed. The next morning Alicia joined us as well. On January 21st, 2017, Donald Trump was being inaugurated as America's new president and there were protest marches world-wide. Jayme's apartment happens to be in midtown Manhattan–right at the start of the Women's March! So I rolled out of bed, coming from the sparse deprivation of West Africa, and opened the door to a sea of pink pussy hats, colorful signs, and sensory overload.

I almost wanted to turn around and retreat back into the cozy confines of the apartment. But Jayme and Alicia gently nudged me forward asking, "Are you going to be okay?"

I had been practicing turning fear stories into love really hardcore on the pilgrimage. All kinds of challenges came up, but none bigger than a very dark force threatening to turn back decades of civil rights progress within a few years. I had been practicing compassion for President Trump because the people who inflict the most harm on others are really the ones who are suffering the most.

But I felt overwhelmed by the energy of the Women's March, and I stuck with it to try and understand it. I marched while practicing presence, breathing, creating an energetic shield, as well as opening up to the powerful love I was witnessing in all the fish swimming in the protest sea. There were so many agendas represented on the day of the March with next to no violence. At first, I was confused what the exact point of the March was—women's rights, immigrants, #blacklivesmatter, environmental protection—pretty much any cause you could think of was cleverly represented on a sign. And people were laughing and high-fiving one another. They were applauding each other's creativity and commitment. People amassed all over the planet to support one another. This March wasn't about our accidental president or even America as an individual nation—it was about a global shift in consciousness.

The "Women's March" was quite possibly the largest and most peaceful in U.S. history (with an estimated 3.3 million people and zero arrests!?) It inspired people worldwide. This inauguration really forced people to reflect on their values, to stand up for beliefs that they are unwilling to allow a bully to threaten. If we stand up together in the spirit we were able to summon on that day, we will surely find our strength.

The irony of a collective is that it takes every individual to make it possible. So, it is up to you, to every individual, to live our lives in ways that are mindful and connected. To ride on the energy of the March to new levels of empowerment and more depth of care. To approach every day as if we could greet our neighbor, show support for someone who needs it, and express what is important to us in creative and uplifting ways. I was astounded by the collective capacity on that day of the March and the willingness to look at this story with love and peace.

Because it's not about any one of us; it's about what is best for all, everywhere.

What is the opposite of caring only about ourselves? It is caring about others. This isn't about a clown in a silly wig who cares more about tv ratings than leading a democratic nation; this isn't about building any more walls that block us off from our humanity. This is about standing side by side until we cover this big beautiful planet with the peace that comes from love and acceptance. It is about letting in what feels outside us so that we can find the love within.

Journeying On

Revisit your original intentions and let them reorganize your energy. Cultivate the courage to express what is in your heart. If you do it with love, in a way that is unifying, I do believe you'll be supported by something greater. In that way, we all will.

Don't get trumped by anything! You have an elixir to bring back that will save us all!

It's the final leg, so give it your all. In Japanese, there is a saying: *ganbatte!* It means something akin to "Give it your all!" or "Do your best!" It means you can do it because you can if you go for it.

You can do it and I look forward to reuniting back in Ordinary World!!

Chapter 12
YOU ARE BEING GUIDED

"Space: the final frontier. These are the voyages of the starship Enterprise. Its five-year mission: to explore strange new worlds, to seek out new life and new civilizations, to boldly go where no man has gone before."

—Captain James T. Kirk, *Star Trek*

Resurrection

We have begun our ascension on the airplane ride that will bring us back to our home airport. We have set out on the road which will guide us back home to unpack. We are headed into the final days of this pilgrimage–as non-linear and as slowed down as time may have seemed. It is all relative. And here we go as we relate to each other on this journey back into Ordinary World.

A curtain of melancholy hangs in the air in this suction chamber of an airplane ride home. But fear not, for when you land in Ordinary World, you are changed. Turn on your overhead reading light and snuggle in your window seat. You are now flying business class. Revel in your coming Resurrection!

Superfriends

Wonder Woman is an Amazonian goddess who descends into "Man's World" in an attempt to restore peace. She is in the world but not of the world. She possesses immeasurable power and shows society a new kind of superhero—one who can triumph without force or firepower, but rather, with love.

She is guided by an energy far superior than any magic powers the gods can yield. Her commitment to compassion and her faith in humanity are what cause her to be one of the strongest superheroes in the Universe.

Your Hero's Journey: Final Attempt / Last-Minute Dangers

What is faith and why do we need it?

Faith is a set of beliefs one has about what one can trust. Some have faith in a higher power. Others have faith in their own abilities. Still others have faith in external sources like science, other people, or the law of cause and effect because they perceive: "When I do A, B happens. It's always the case. I can trust in that."

But when it comes down to it, everyone has faith in *something*. Even if you are a nihilist: you have faith in nothing. That's your belief you can trust in.

There are as many spiritual paths as there are people on this planet. As my teacher, Venerable Dzigar Kongtrul Rinpoche, advised me: "You can either commit to a spiritual path (with guidance from a teacher) or a personal path. But you need to choose."

You can choose to be a devout disciple of God or you can choose to use scientific discovery to fuel your beliefs. You can pray to the Hindu gods or you can use your life experience as spiritual proof. You can experiment in a lab, on the cushion, or in your life to find out what works with repeated results and what doesn't. I would encourage you to never take the "easy" path of blind faith, either spiritual or scientific, without testing it out with a healthy dose of skepticism. A true skeptic questions the truth of something but is able to adapt their opinion when the proof presents itself.

To shed the beliefs that were handed to us and make our own discoveries is the way to our freedom.

Writing Opportunity! What do you believe to be true?

We live in an incredible age of information and technology. You can find evidence to support any belief by typing it into Google or aligning with like-minded people through meet-ups and chat rooms. What it boils down to is what you choose to believe. So, if you don't know what to believe, pick any one! See if it works for you. Stick with it past the point that feels comfortable and choose something new if it is leading you back down the false path of darkness.

Another secret: *any* path will lead you to where you want to go. The story structure is the same no matter what the circumstances. You now know how the story goes. Use it to test the next phase of your life, your current beliefs, and everything that arises as obstacles and miracles.

You can learn what you need from sticking with one path. There is a phenomenon of "spiritual shopping" that can happen when we try something and it doesn't serve our pre-existing *false* belief system. We want the world to agree with us and hand us everything we want without needing to do the hard work of transformation. If you've made it this far in the journey, I don't think that applies to you. But notice in yourself: do you bail out when the going gets tough? Would you rather lie around and do nothing, waiting for someone to save you? Do you jump from one teacher/practice/belief system hoping to be saved from something or someone outside yourself?

If so, the bad news is: You'll have to give that up. Only you have the power and inner wisdom to save yourself.

The good news: There's help!

We live in an inextricably interconnected universe. This is a long-standing spiritual belief; quantum physics is proving how complex this interconnected web is. In fact, it's very simple: Separation is something we create in our minds.

It is possible to surrender that idea as well, that *you* need to do everything or it will all fall apart. The Universe is just fine, thank you. It is also willing to be in complete collaboration if you so choose.

It's a paradox: You are in complete control *and* you have control over nothing.

Here's how I resolve that: You have complete control over your inner world: what you choose to believe, and how you can literally transform your entire being by attending to your thoughts, feelings, and behaviors. You can build new neural pathways in your brain that impact your physical body (from your appearance down to your genetic make-up) to the world that you create around you. Your source is all there is.

What power!

What is equally as powerful and equally ignored in most people's lives is surrendering that whole inner world to an external force. This is truly the final step of creating the world you want to see. If you want a new job, new apartment, to stop fighting with your mother, or to go to Peru like you've always wanted, you can think about it all you want. But there are an infinite amount of causes and conditions that will cause these things to manifest. You're not in control of any of those.

But *something* is. *Something* is holding this all together and generating this glorious field of possibility turned reality. You will more quickly get what you want by giving it up to this force.

This is getting your ego out of the way and letting the Universe take the wheel.

I find great power in knowing that I have everything I need to fly this plane, and at the same time, I can put it on cruise control and glide easily to where I need to go. We built this sophisticated transportation system together. That means I can be here now and relax in this luminous moment now.

Here are the Manifestation Steps on Your Heart Path:

1. Thinking
2. Feeling
3. Acting
4. Being
5. Co-creating

1. You have to recognize the patterns in your thinking that are causing you pain. Then, you need to acknowledge what you really want. Thought brings you what you desire.

2. You need to feel into these thoughts. You need to feel into the pain of staying small and stuck. And then be willing to let that go. Then, feel into the joy and glory of your desires.

Every time you notice yourself slipping into the old way of thinking, make a choice to think again. Think the way you want. Then, feel into that. Emotion creates stronger vibrations in the quantum field.

3. Act the way you want to feel. Take inspired action. Action allows you to receive that which you think into form.

4. Be the person you want to be before you see results. The quantum field needs some time to reorganize around this new you.

5. Get in communication with the Universe and let it go. Some call this "prayer." I like to have a conversation with the quantum field. Tell it what you want. It only wants you to be happy. Then, stop controlling *how* it's going to happen. The Universe knows better than any one of us. It has an intelligence that expands to infinity. Let it use some of its resources to create miracles in your life.

It goes back to your unique path. You've created this path by developing neural networks in your mind. They manifest as the habitual patterns that show up in your life. So what are yours?

Writing Opportunity! Do you tend to rely on your own willpower or do you give over too easily to belief systems and ideas? Are you more prone to action or inaction? Do you commit to things easily or are you resistant to commitment? Looking at your personal patterns reveals a world of spiritual truth.

My Resurrection

I share this with you because I let fear lead my own life for so many years. I relied on my own willpower and overcommitted myself to just about everything. I'm an artist at heart and constantly inspired. So I was constantly doing things, anything. And I was burning out on a consistent cycle as well. I am also innately curious so I explored so many passions and spiritual paths. In a way, there is nothing wrong with this. If not for my multi-passionate nature, I wouldn't be able to write this story today. But there comes a point when we must recognize that our patterns are precisely what are causing us pain. Being overcommitted to too many things left me fully committed to none. I was not an attentive friend or partner. I avoided finishing projects because shiny objects caught my eye and dragged me away. I did not fully understand myself until I recognized my own patterns and gave them up. I committed to one spiritual path that allows me to take in the entirety of the universe. That said, everything is a paradox! I deeply study and practice Tibetan Buddhism, and also practice energy healing and Kundalini yoga. I am super into Jesus again and love learning about the connective threads between all spiritual teachings. I make art, write, teach, coach, dance, podcast, build temples, commune with animals, inspire humans, and beyond. You, too, can do anything and everything you love. But you must choose love over fear. And you must commit fully to whatever path speaks to your heart. You must do this despite what the conventional world will tell you, and instead, create the world you want to see.

This is how you will get out of your office and into your life–living and loving it beyond your wildest dreams.

When you surrender to faith, you never know how it will turn out. For many, this is terrifying. Therefore, the ego snaps into control mode. However, if you can manage to quiet down that voice which seeks to keep you small, you will find that the universe always has a better plan.

Without us humans mucking things up, nature is abundant. Trees lose their leaves and they regrow. They don't worry about what anyone is going to think of them. They simply do what they are meant to do. Be abundant. Serve the ecosystem. Participate in the cycles of death and rebirth over and over again. You are no different than those trees, though your ego would have you believe differently. As the acorn grows into the mighty oak, there is also a plan for you.

Are you ready to stop resisting and grow into your destiny?

When I completed the Shikoku Pilgrimage on universal time, I didn't really know what to expect after. But I had heard stories.

Jyana, for example, had completed five days of the pilgrimage. (Since there is no set way to do it, like all good paths, one can start Shikoku in any number of places or finish in any number of ways.) After five days, she received her PhD funding to stay in Tokyo for two more years. She chalked this up to the blessings of Kobo Daishi who had forged the pilgrimage path. As with all formal pilgrimages, there is a promise of merit gained by pursuing this challenging course. This can show up in an infinite number of ways.

I was excited to see how it was going to show up for me!

I miraculously met up with Yamamoto-san at Temple #88. We had traveled together briefly when he had coerced me into taking the bus on that particularly rainy day. We then parted ways, interested in different kinds of adventure. I wanted to stay on for hot springs, rest, and exploration of the "big city" of Matsuyama. Yamamoto-san wanted to push forward to complete it on his own timeframe. I needed the self-care; he needed to push forward. We kindly parted ways, only to meet up again, finishing at exactly the same time.

As my bus guru, he informed me that the only bus down to the main city left soon after I had arrived. If I missed that bus, I would miss my train and ferry to Naoshima. I hurried to recite the Heart Sutra and make offerings at the end of this intense journey.

I barely made the bus and plopped down next to Yamamoto-san. I checked my cell phone for the first time in days, only to receive a nasty email from someone dear to me. We had recently had a falling out, but I had been so moved by the challenges of pilgrimage that I figured: *How much harder could the challenge of forgiveness be?* I asked him if I could make prayers for him, but hadn't heard back from him before the final temple. So I made a prayer for his happiness and wellbeing. Upon receiving his unhappy message, I figured I had made the right prayer after all. I prayed again for his happiness, and for mine.

Then, I started to get really itchy. My right arm was *itchyyyyy! Supaa Kayuii!* I mentioned this to Yamamoto-san and showed him my arm, which was rapidly developing a red rash over my entire forearm. Yamamoto-san happened to have an anti-itch potion that he quickly handed over and told me I could keep. Then he gave me some Japanese crackers. I felt like this was my consolation prize. *Jyana got her PhD funding and I get a poisonous rash???*

How about that for merit?

But a true Hero continues on despite adversity, so I went to Naoshima and had a wonderful time soaking in environmental sculpture, hot springs, and the sea spray on the beach outside my yurt. Several people were alarmed by the intensity of my rash and insisted I go to a doctor. But I only had three days to enjoy my life. I told them that I would go if it got worse. So, I practiced peaceful co-existence with the rash, applying the magic potion gift from Yamamoto-san. I didn't scratch it despite an overwhelming desire to be free from the pain. I watched it carefully as it morphed back into new skin, free from irritation. I noticed a corresponding peacefulness take over my heart as well.

And then I went on with my life. I met Stephanie in Tokyo. Alicia and I traveled to Aomori. Then I returned to the U.S. to do reconnaissance on my life that had burned to ashes.

The thing is, once you go on a journey like this, and you let what's not serving you burn away, you can't go back to who you were before. That person and those places no longer exist. And so I was reborn from the ashes like the mighty phoenix. I returned home with my elixir of anti-itch potion. (My mother used the rest on our dog, which seemed to help with her allergic skin condition as well.)

Now, you may be nearing the end of this book journey, and wondering what you've learned and how it will manifest. Will you use the process outlined herein to manifest riches? Or are there more itchy rashes you must face before you return home with the tools to master creating a new world?

Either way, I encourage you to be kind. Be patient. It's about the journey, not the destination. And the journey happens again and again, until infinity.

I have one final tale for the time being. I hope it will help you let go of any ego that wants to know how it will turn out, instead of relaxing into this final phase. Because when we get on the path and start collaborating with universal forces, we never do know how it will turn out. I can promise you, however, that it will be more fantastical than we are capable of imagining.

Fast forward to July 2016. It's two years after I completed the Shikoku Pilgrimage. I am at our Buddhist *sangha's* yearly retreat teachings. William and Mariko are having a wedding ceremony one evening and we all attend.

Afterwards, Sarah and I are walking down to the outhouses. Gretchen is my teacher's assistant and she is running up the hill.

"Get down there!" she exclaims. "Rinpoche is alone in the field–go keep him company!"

Our esteemed teacher got to the party early. We ran down to join him.

Turns out, he was not alone. He was standing there with Dai-san who was visiting from Japan. Kongtrul Rinpoche introduces me to Dai-san since I have Japanese heritage. We come to discuss how I completed the Shikoku Pilgrimage in June 2014.

"Whaaaaaaaat?!" Dai-san exclaims. "When did you go??"

"I started in May 2014, during the rainy season when no one in their right minds would go."

"Whaaaaat… I brought Rinpoche to Shikoku for the first time in May 2014, right before the rainy season. He was there and then you came. That's amazing!!!"

The way I ended up helping build Kongtrul Rinpoche's temple in Colorado is a whole other fantastical story. But in that moment, I knew that my teacher had called me from afar. It was as if he had sprinkled fairy dust on that island. I had inhaled it and it led me to a remote part of Colorado to find my destiny. I wouldn't be doing the work I am doing if I hadn't made my way there.

This is how merit shows up–in ways more miraculous and unbelievable than life generally allows. It is clearly the work of a power both in our control, and way, way beyond.

Journeying On

You never know how it's going to turn out. But I've laid out the steps in the previous chapters, the ones you can take to embark on your own Hero's Journey. It will allow you to leave the life you once knew, and be a conscious creator of a magical new one.

We create from our source–the one that exists both within and without. The creative power is truly all you need to find your calling, pay your bills, and live a life of purpose.

"Professionally things are really shaking up! With work, I feel more competent, useful, and appreciated. I realize where I can make an impact in this business and am excited with how it can evolve. I'm grateful because I feel more stabilized with my income and my boss and the other project managers feel more confident in my work and show gratitude for what I bring to the table–even if it's just good energy! And I love it because when I wake up, I don't have that sad feeling of having to go to work, instead I embrace it with a smile. When I was back home for my nephew's birthday, I got to go when I wanted without requesting time off, I did some work remotely of course, and coming back home wasn't this 'oh well, back to the grind' ho hum Eeyore sullenness. That is gone. I'm able to wake and do things like my morning pages, play a song, or cuddle a few

minutes longer, according to my schedule, not someone else's. And that feels AWESOME! I'm doing by doing me!"

—**Stephanie Juen**, Virtual Pilgrim

Conclusion

GO FORTH AND
SHINE YOUR LIGHT!

"We shall not cease from exploration, and the end of all our exploring will be to arrive where we started and know the place for the first time."

—T. S. Eliot

Return with Elixir

Welcome home, dear one. It is with the utmost gratitude and outstretched arms that I welcome you back from your journey.

It's a leap of faith to pick up a book like this one, to go down to the stormy basement of *The NeverEnding Story*, to fight The Nothing with only a candle to light the way. It's difficult to know you only have an apple to eat and trust that food will show up when you need it. To snuggle yourself into your blanket of self-care and to enter into a tale that was once reserved in secret until you were ready. It is no small feat to go on a journey of this kind. But you have done it. I salute you.

What you have learned, by delving into this timeless tale, has the potential to shape the rest of your life. It has the potential to shape the world as we know it. We went on a Hero's Journey to reprogram the inner workings of our mind; we busted through the major myths of the material world to create a new story. I have purposefully given you a lot because I know you can take your torch forward into the world. It shines brighter than ever before. I have faith that you can use it to illuminate the darkness we face and make the world a brighter and better place. If you ever need help navigating the shadows, you know where to find me.

You've been given the tools to go inward and find mystical worlds within. The mysteries of human consciousness are yours to explore and you can repeat the Hero's Journey time and time again. Inherent in the process is the necessity of repetition. Like an onion, we peel away layers of our psyche to reveal other stinky fearful layers underneath. We keep peeling them away until we get to the core of our being. When we go through the cycles of purification and accumulation enough times, we will transcend this world completely. We will be fully enlightened. The worldly suffering will cause us pain no more. When we can reprogram all of the neural connections that have been created based on fear, we are free to create fully and completely from love. When we can accomplish this as a human collective, the entire world as we know it will become enlightened as well.

Until that time, we do exist here in this material realm. In the chaos and confusion of the current moment, we need a spiritual practice. Technology is evolving at an exponential rate. We need to learn how to slow down and be in the now while The Nothing's darkness threatens to overcome us and annihilate us all. We need a solid foundation we can fall back on when times get tough, and they *will* get tough. We need to get tougher. And we do that by softening, by surrendering to a power that has the ability to heal, grow, and create.

Reality is not as real as it seems. By rewiring your neural connections, you create new ones that communicate with a quantum system of support. When we are able to let go into the wonder and magnificence of this universal life energy, we fall in love with the world again. This is what it means to be truly living in this life, in this moment. We create and destroy in a constant cycle of life. When we can do this with love, when we are able to consciously create our world with the help of universal guidance, we are able to transcend.

It is my wish for you that you take what you have discovered here and return home, to share your gifts with the world. By reading these words, you are more expanded than when you began. By taking the writing opportunities to face your fears, you are all the more ready to let love in. By developing your own meditation practice, you are ready to share your peace of mind with others. You can follow your vision to the life you want to lead, and you will lead others to do the same by your heroic example. It is an exciting moment to own your mastery, embrace your gifts, and heed your true calling. There is a job for you to do–you are meant to shine your light into the world.

> *"There is nothing enlightened about shrinking so that other people won't feel insecure around you. We are all meant to shine, as children do. We were born to make manifest the glory of God that is within us. It's not just in some of us; it's in everyone. And as we let our own light shine, we unconsciously give other people permission to do the same. As we are liberated from our own fear, our presence automatically liberates others."*
> —**Marianne Williamson**, *A Return to Love*

One of the most notable transformations for Virtual Pilgrims is the call to serve. Facing our fears opens us up to love in a new way, a new definition. Gone is the attachment to a conception of romantic love as the ultimate form and we arrive at an unconditional state of being that is true love.

> *"Love actually does heal. There's a biological reason it heals. It creates what is called 'limbic resonance' in your brain and it starts self-repair mechanisms. In medicine we call this 'homeostasis'–it takes you back to your original state, which is wellbeing."*
> **—Deepak Chopra**

May this book serve as a guide to spread your love out to heal the world and to be of service to the greater good. This book contains the necessary instructions to set you on a new journey–and a map for when you get lost. You can choose to embark on your new adventure solo like I did when I went to Shikoku. You can do all this work on your own and emerge victorious. But I can tell you this from experience, it is a much easier journey when you find new friends! We humans are mirrors for each other. Our learning increases exponentially when we do it together. As individuals, we are able to create homes. As a collective, we create societies.

It took me a very long time to accept my own role as a change-maker. It took burning through lifetimes of false beliefs to understand that I truly do co-create with the quantum field. I am still in this process, and I share it with you because I have a big dream for a better future. I dream that all beings attain enlightenment; in this physical realm, it means that all beings experience deep and abiding peace and prosperity. I have touched the future. It is now.

I had to take a huge leap to get here. I was deep into studying and practicing Tibetan Vajrayana Buddhism. I had experiences where Sacred

World melded with this one. However, when it came to some of my most stubborn, deep-rooted blocks, I had to burn through them like the fires of hell. It was really painful. I had to give more and more until I thought I could give no more. I had to let go of my safe problems, and step up and address the real ones.

One of my biggest stuck places is around Money. (Believe me, I have suffered from all three, as noted in the previous tales.) But growing up with an immigrant mother, we heard tales of hardship since before we were even born. It was imprinted on us to equate money with hardship. My mother's mantras for us included sayings like "Get a husband and a good job and take care of your parents when we are old." My father was mostly gone, working through most of our existence. My dad was an entrepreneur who taught me the meaning in hard work; his work was his primary focus. This gave me a killer work ethic, but I also inherited many false ideas about money that caused me to work myself nearly to death and caused problems in my relationships with others. These false beliefs limited what I was capable of creating, until I decided to look at them for what they really were–nothing.

So while I was planning to go on the pilgrimage to India, I had to come up with the funds to do so. And I *had* to go on the pilgrimage to India. Right before it was announced, I met with my spiritual teacher, Kongtrul Rinpoche. In that meeting, I asked him if he would ever lead another pilgrimage to the Buddha's holy sites. I had heard tales from many of the senior members in our Buddhist sangha about times long past and the glory of going on pilgrimage with our dear teacher. I had heard that voice again, urging me to ask him about the future possibility.

"Well, actually, I asked Jampal to lead the pilgrimage again. So there is that opportunity."

Dungse Jampal Norbu is my teacher's son and dharma heir. I serendipitously already had scheduled a meeting with him two days later. Upon seeing him, he enthusiastically announced that he would be leading the *Dana Pilgrimage* again in November. My fate was sealed. I had asked for this. It was given to me. (Please note: this is exactly how manifesting happens. When you don't take what is being offered out of fear, the Universe thinks you must not want it and will stop presenting you with what you want. So you bet I signed up for that pilgrimage as soon as possible.)

But then, I had to raise the funds to go. It was not cheap with airfare, costs covering the pilgrimage, offerings, hotels, etc. And I was making barely enough to buy food on a normal day. My old foe Money Monster raised its ugly head.

But beauty is in the eye of the beholder, and I resolved to heal our relationship once and for all.

Through the magic of social media, I received a Twitter message from Vibeke Schurch about manifesting money and an offer for a free alignment session. Mind you, I wasn't really on Twitter at all. I don't know if I had ever checked a Direct Message. But something, that whispering voice, told me to click the button. Thus, I did. I completed her 5-day "Manifest Your Dream Clients" Challenge. I immediately got on the phone with her. I knew mid-way through speaking with her that she would become my first-ever coach. At that time, I didn't even really know what a coach was.

Cue: Vibeke. I knew we were destined to work together. Her fees, however, were way beyond what I could even conceive of making. Not to mention the new pilgrimage dues on their way to my credit card. But it felt right. It felt like there must be a way out. And there was.

Because of my work with Vibeke, I created the Virtual Pilgrim Course. She encouraged me to create the dream that was in my heart. I said, "I'm going on a pilgrimage in less than a month. And I want to bring people with me virtually. I want them to feel like they are on the pilgrimage without ever needing to leave home. I want to take people on a creative and spiritual virtual journey that would help them transform their lives."

I didn't know where that came from and immediately tried to take it back. I had no idea what I even meant! Furthermore, how the heck was I going to transport people through time and space virtually?? But Vibeke did not let me back down from my dreams. That's part of what a good coach does.

I'll be honest–I was surprised that people agreed to do something so bizarre! But I had a group of incredible souls who not only helped me fund my spiritual journey, but they went with me. Astounding, miraculous transformations occurred. If it weren't for my intrepid Virtual Pilgrims, I couldn't have gone on the journey at all. And if I didn't have the guts to take that chance, I wouldn't have created something that would touch people's lives so deeply. The transformations I witnessed changed my own life. That one move inspired this book, and will continue to impact the lives of many others.

Should I have given up on the dream in my heart because it didn't seem possible? Looking back, I would have never chosen anything other than this path. Here's another big secret: You don't have to know *how*. You only have to know *what* dream is in your heart. If you act in alignment with the *what* and the *why*, the universe happily takes care of the how. What a great relief! Going through the Manifestation Steps means that you can check a huge part of your To Do List off and delegate those tasks to a force that knows better. That force can make things happen in ways we could never imagine.

You can struggle and try to control the outcomes. Or you can let the glory of god guide you. The choice is yours: struggle, pain, lack, despair. Or: ease, radiant wellbeing, abundance, joy.

All you have to do is claim your reward.

I spent many years trying to figure things out "on my own." I wouldn't pay for courses because I was steeped in lack mentality. *Why pay for something you can do on your own?* The thought of paying someone to help me seemed so far out of reach even if I wanted it. But after working with my first coach, I wouldn't do it any other way. After seeing the transformations my Virtual Pilgrims went through, I will forever help others to achieve their own dreams.

Working with others shakes up the fabric of time and gives us energy combined towards a common goal. So if you want to go bigger and make a global impact with your work, let's form a collective. We can be like the X-Men or the Justice League, working on a freer world for all.

The Virtual Pilgrimage has now expanded into my signature program, The Hero's Way. This course combines all the mind training and energy work from the Virtual Pilgrimage needed to bust through the false myths that are holding us back. It also provides heroes-in-training with the complete set of skills to manifest abundance. On returning to Ordinary World, participants leave with a Treasure Map to Abundance–a fully aligned business plan that will allow them to phase out of their current jobs and into careers they love that save the world. Together, we create a no-fail plan because what we are actually doing is going into business with the Universe itself.

Who wouldn't want to start their business with the Universe as an investor?

The most exciting part is that it includes both virtual *and* live pilgrimages! We are forming a mighty tribe of like-spirited heroes. Together, I believe we will actually save the world.

Are you *in*???

If so, I would love for you to share any breakthroughs you've had during this journey. Please do stay in touch. I would love to hear where you are on your journey. We can talk about the best way for you to wormhole directly to your dreams.

"My love radiates from me like light from a bonfire—focused on none, and denied to none."

—**Nisargadatta Maharaj**

The fire never ceases and the journey never ends! If you want it to continue immediately, join me at BecomeYourHero.com for an amazing opportunity to transcend time and space, and create a whole new world with me. (That's the last movie reference you'll get unless you answer the call to adventure again!)

READING LIST

Slipstream Time Hacking by Benjamin Hardy
Must read this book. It's a game-changer.

The 4-Hour Work Week by Timothy Ferriss
Also a game-changer.

How to Quit Your Job—The Right Way: A 5-Step Plan to Ditching Your Day Job by Danny Iny and Jim Hopkinson
When you are ready to make the leap.

The Seven Spiritual Laws of Success by Deepak Chopra
"According to the book, when we comprehend and apply these laws in our lives, everything we want can be created, 'because the same laws that nature uses to create a forest, a star, or a human body can also bring about the fulfillment of our deepest desires.'" (Wikipedia)

The Science of Getting Rich by Wallace D. Wattles

+

The Abundance Book by John Randolph Price

+

Think and Grow Rich by Napoleon Hill

=

If you want to manifest abundance in your life, I recommend these books together. The Abundance Book, in particular, has a 40-day practice for manifesting abundance.

Abundance: The Future is Better Than You Think by Peter Diamandis
    and Steven Kotler
For socially-conscious big picture thinking in tech, culture, business, and worldview. Proof that the future is now.

Breaking the Habit of Being Yourself by Dr. Joe Dispenza

It's Up to You by Dzigar Kongtrül Rinpoche

When Things Fall Apart by Pema Chödrön

Shambhala: The Sacred Path of the Warrior by Chögyam Trungpa

The Universe Has Your Back: Turn Your Fear to Faith by Gabrielle
    Bernstein

Big Magic by Elizabeth Gilbert

The Desire Map by Danielle Laporte

The Artist's Way by Julia Cameron

ACKNOWLEDGMENTS

Writing this book was an epic Hero's Journey unto itself. There are so many allies and mentors who helped guide me to Special World and back. Even when I had to go inward and face the deepest caves of my own fears, I was never truly alone. What a gift you are for being alive. My heart is exploding with gratitude.

Thank you to the intrepid Virtual Pilgrims who trusted me to take them beyond the realms of the Ordinary before it was even clear exactly what that meant! Kim Woodcock, Lisa Gay Gardner, Alicia Remolde, Carol Rosenfeld, Stephanie Juen, Nathan Sutton, and Jimena Duca–without you, none of this would have been possible. It has evolved beyond my wildest dreams and your faith kept me accountable to the transformation.

My collaborators Jayme Jennings, Miyu Leilani, Daniel Munkus, and Axel Jenson, you came on this journey with me in so many ways. Your commitment to creativity and kindness carried me through murky places where I would have surely sank elsewise. I know our creativity and spirit will continue to shine together in new ways as we continue on.

To my sage mentors who guided my writing and empowered my creative spirit: Angela Lauria and Vibeke Schurch. Your coaching made me realize that it's not about the book, business, or any other material thing—it's about becoming the person I'm meant to be. That person is meant to serve the world. I learn more about who that might be on a daily basis. May that person go on to inspire countless others to reach their highest potential.

Anna Paradox, could a more aligned editor ever have manifested? Thanks to your vast experience, kind heart, and deep understanding, this book emerged from many dark nights of the soul and into the light. You are a breath of fresh air and I shout many thanks to you from the mountaintops!

To the Morgan James Publishing team: Special thanks to David Hancock, CEO & Founder for believing in me and my message. To my Author Relations Manager, Margo Toulouse, thanks for making the process seamless and easy. Many more thanks to everyone else, but especially Jim Howard, Bethany Marshall, and Nickcole Watkins.

Lisa Levine, I would be nothing if I didn't understand energy. Your smile and radiant wisdom continue to guide me to the light of love.

Gabrielle Bernstein, you were my Virtual Mentor. I thank the Universe that it brought me to your work. It really does have my back, and with your guidance, taught me to transform my fear to faith.

Carol Rosenfeld, my very first mentor, dear friend, and Virtual Companion, thank you for asking me "Have you written your book yet?" Post-Pilgrimage, this was exactly what I needed to hear. Thank you for your endless curiosity and questioning.

I am incredibly honored to have been accepted and uplifted by the Mangala Shri Bhuti sangha early on in this journey. It is so important to have a spiritual community to catch us when we fall down on the path.

I am indebted to everyone in this community, and especially those who provided me with shelter, care, and the wings to fly. When I appeared in your realm, I was a hot mess. Chaos is par for the course, but you helped me find the ground from which I could soar. Joey, Vanessa and Lila Waxman, Rowen Hurley, Sarah Bennett, Nicholas and Natasha Carter, Judith Brown-Meyers, Susan Walp, Helen Connole, Sasha and Tatjana Krizmanic Meyerowitz, Caroline Bliss-Kandel, Pat Noyes, Michael Velasco, Clare and Dana Ming, and John and Bayard Cobb– you continue to create the space for my creations to come to life again and again. Ani Pema Chödrön, thank you for telling me to build that temple, even though you didn't necessarily know you were doing it.

Sue Cummings, thank you for driving me to free the lobsters that would heal my heart. I promise to pay it forward a million times over.

Jyana and Earl Browne, your wisdom and intuition led me on the journey to inspire many journeys to come. You get any merit I may have accidentally accumulated. Many blessings to all the Pilgrimage Angels I have met along the way.

I would literally not be here without my sweet and wacky family: John, Sumi, and Alicia. Thank you for encouraging me to follow my dreams and for continuing to expand with me as we all grow. It is an indescribable delight to be so in love with the family who has borne me. I am equally grateful to my found family of friends and furballs who light up my life. You are my companions on life's journey, a great comfort and joy through the darkness and the light.

Last but certainly not least, tremendous gratitude to my Buddhist teachers Venerable Dzigar Kongtrul Rinpoche, Elizabeth Mattis-Namgyel and Dungse Jampal Norbu–for calling me from afar, being spiritual activists, and guiding pilgrimage with such grace. You teach me to walk the spiritual path in my life. May this book and all continued action be a benefit to all beings.

ABOUT THE AUTHOR

 Sophia Remolde has lived many lifetimes within this one, and inspires the emerging heroes of this world to experience and cultivate the great joy of transformation. Sophia is a multi-prismatic artist, energy healer, wormhole coach, wordsmith, and lobsterbird. By bridging our polarities, bringing together that which seemingly cannot co-exist, we experience deep peace and radiant transcendence. This work allows the spark of creativity to ignite and feed the flames of a forest fire of enlightenment.

Sophia has studied everything from psychology and creativity to art and spirituality. She holds an MFA in Performance and Interactive Media Arts, and her thesis *Robot Immigrants* chronicled her mother's story through robotics and Butoh dance. This led her on a journey to investigate the importance of our personal stories and how to apply them in a spiritual and universal perspective. Traveling the world as a nomadic pilgrim, Sophia spends half her time creating Energy Art and working on Compassionate Social Action projects. The other half is devoted to The Hero's Way, guiding other heroes to find work they love that changes the world.

Our true treasure lies within the creative potential of our own minds; it is through collaboration with the quantum field that we bring this treasure to life. Because the quantum field is the source of unlimited potentialities, the work takes a plethora of forms.

You can explore some of them here: sophiaremolde.com + lobsterbird.com

THANK YOU

Congratulations, Hero!

You made it all the way to Special World and back, bringing home the magical elixir that will help you transform the world you once knew. Thank you for joining me on this journey, and for your commitment to creating a better world for all.

As you continue the journey, new adventures are in store. In order to aid you on your heroic quest, I've created a free **Hero Mastery Training** especially for you! This video transmission will beam me into your current headquarters so we can devise a plan to save the day. We will go deeper into busting the Myths of Ordinary World so you can find freedom and alignment doing work you love. You will learn to Create Cash Flow in Collaboration with the Quantum Field to aid you on your mission to save the world.

Travel over to **BecomeYourHero.com** to begin a new journey and take charge of your destiny.

And if you know you are ready to seriously step out and save the world, come join me on The Hero's Way! Visit **BecomeYourHero.com/ apply** to join a superhero collective creating a world of abundance and love for all.

Big love to you, my Superfriend!

xx Sophi-Lobsterbird

Morgan James
Speakers Group

www.TheMorganJamesSpeakersGroup.com

We connect Morgan James published
authors with live and online events
and audiences who will benefit
from their expertise.

Morgan James makes all of our titles available
through the Library for All Charity Organization.

www.LibraryForAll.org